Peter Anderson

It must have been a difficult task to write The Jam's biog - there haven't been any drug busts, violent deaths or mystical sojourns. Things that seemed vital to us may sound trivial to other people.

For instance my fondest memory of The Jam and the most important time for the group and me was the hours we spent travelling up and down the motorway in a Ford Transit. All quite Billy Fury filmish really but...

Either way there is no more to be said on The Jam's formation and the rise than is contained in this book.

P.W. June 1983

Chris Clunn

Paolo Hewitt, like a lot, was born in 1958 on the 11th of July. Although born in England, his ancenstory traces back to Naples and the Italian ghettos of New York. After completing secondary school, he went for trials at Tottenham Hotspur Football Club, getting through to the last five but eventually deciding, as he could see the sport getting really trendy amongst the hoi polloi, to try his hand in the world of literature. Unsurprisingly, he has proved to be enormously successful.

His first endeavour was a book of short stories entitled, *Bless The Reason Why* which was only published in Italy where it remains in the top ten to this day. Music being his other inspiration, he secured jobs with both Melody Maker and NME where his keen sense of style and similies caused major fits amongst his Oxfam clad co-workers. Where others would be pining to put The Student Bikers on the front cover, or apply situationist theories to situations they knew nothing about, Paolo would be insisting on all expense paid trips to New York or Ibiza to cover his fave Rap or House bands and get a nice tan in the process. His instincts, as ever, proved to be 100% correct.

When he bored of the colour of his desk, he disappeared from view to write a mod novel, *Heaven's Promise* (Heavenly) and a major biography of The Small Faces entitled *The Young Mod's Forgotten Story* (Acid Jazz). He is currently writing pieces on Northern Soul, Oasis, walruses and other Mod related subjects. He may publish them, he may not. But one thing is for sure. Paolo still lives in London, is single, and still has beautiful eyes!

Colonel Boogie writes again, 1996.

THE JAM
a beat concerto

By Paolo Hewitt

BØXTREE

First published in the UK in 1983 by
Book Sales Ltd
78, Newman Street
London W1P 3LA

Revised Edition first published in the UK in 1996 by
Boxtree Ltd
21 Broadwall
London SE1 9PL

In association with
Go! Discs
72 Black Lion Lane
London W6 9BE

Cover design by Simon Halfon, 3 Lions DA

Additional book design by PUSH, London

Cover photo by Andrew Douglas

Printed and bound in Italy by New Interlitho SPA

ISBN: 0 7522 0269 3

Many thanks to the following for:
Editing: Tony Stewart, who turned the bitter into sweet.
Interviews: Paul Weller, Bruce Foxton, Rick Buckler, Ann Weller, John Weller, Steve Carver,
Pete Carver, Mr and Mrs Buckler, Steve Baker, Kenny Wheeler, Steve Brookes and Roger Pilling.
Cuttings and clippings supplied by: Gary Crowley of GLR, The Beat and Browns,
Pete Melon with tapes and fanzines, the Polydor Press office and top artiste Ian Wright.
Tape transcription: Sidekicks Co., Hampstead and top boy, Russell Bacon.
New Edition brought to the top by: Jake Lingwood, out of his Boxtree

Solid Bond Support
The inestimable Paul Weller and his top P&M, Ann and John, Sir Simon Halfon of Swiss Cottage, Stephanie Hardy, Marco
Nelson, the Ocean Colour Scene boys, Jeff and Wendy Barrett, all the Oasis crew plus Meg, Fran and Jess, the boys and girls
of Primal Scream, Tasha Lee and the Heavenly possee, the 67 Leyden boys (Jonesy, Crouch and the Turtle) Pat Stead, Dennis
Munday, Noel Gallagher for his foreword and foresight, Travis Bickle, Johnny Chandler, Gary Crowley, Tony Stewart, Kate
Wills and her famiglia, Pete and Claire Barrett, Andy Mac, Mike Heneghan, Tony Crean, Fergus and all Go! Discs personnel
who have got personal, Eugene Manzi, my good amici, Robert De Niro, plus the top Kiddiwink patrol of Sarah Jane Bacchus,
Jo Jo and Cleo Howard, Nat and Leah Weller, thus the target is made complete.

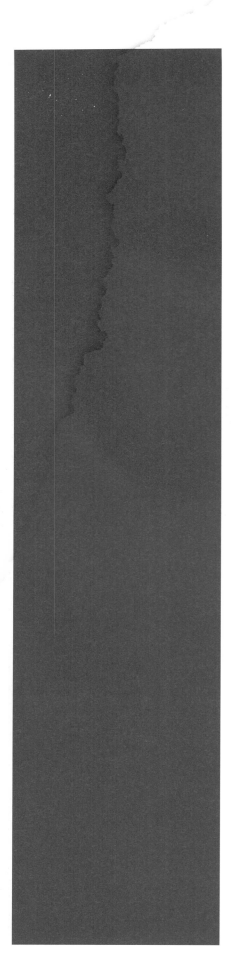

Foreword

I remember when I first heard 'Eton Rifles', my first reaction was, nobody is allowed to be this good. That's how I seriously felt about the record. The Jam were an astonishing group. People go on about how I missed seeing the Beatles live, but the Jam were my Beatles. I saw them loads of times and they rarely turned in a bad show.

I suppose I got into them around about the time of 'Eton Rifles', 1979 time. I saw them on TV, 'So It Goes', I think it was and just the way Paul attacked his guitar, like it was the last time he would ever play it, coupled with this incredible melody, energy and noise, turned me round. I became a real fan of the group, although my favourite album of theirs is not a studio one, but 'Snap', the greatest hits compilation. The song for me has to be 'Tales From The Riverbank', the B-side to 'Absolute Beginners'.

It still knocks me out when I hear it. Paul's ability to conjure up the imagery of the lyrics within the music, plus its real sense of innocence, is the mark of a truly great songwriter. The Jam were a major influence on my own stuff and not just musically. The way they always made sure to put these great B-sides on their records and went out of their way to not rip people off, made The Jam a real people's band. And Paul's insistence on singing in an English working-class voice and never disguising his roots, was another inspiration. Millions of working-class kids loved this group and were inspired by them. I was just one of them. Boss group and a boss book to go with them.

Noel Gallagher, April 1996.

Introduction

Neal Preston

It is impossible to look back at any piece of your own writing without a critical eye. No piece is perfect even if it's only the author who can spot the cracks.

This is a good book, no doubt in my mind on that score, and easily the best published account of The Jam. But re-reading 'A Beat Concerto', twelve years on, my only slight regret is that I was distracted a little by The Jam's huge success. It was that which may have helped me to overlook some real gems ('Liza Radley', 'Shopping', 'Dreams Of Children'), and not give them as much prominence in the book as the obvious songs. It's a tiny regret but then it's always the tiny things that irk the most. Even though they'd been finished for a year by the time I handed in the final manuscript, their name still carried huge weight. They were still being talked about, still being dissected. How Paul Weller could have split them up so casually was a source of great wonderment as was their enormous chart success.

To be honest, this regret was first engendered when I was asked to write the sleeve notes to 'Extras', a 1992 Jam compilation of demos, unreleased songs and album tracks. Listening to that album, which is actually my favourite Jam album, I was forcefully reminded not only of Paul Weller's abilities, but the unremarked upon musical sources that he has drawn from. The Jam covered a lot of ground in their time, some of it really obvious (pop, r'n'b), and other areas

which were not. Listening to ' No One In The World', for example, brings to mind the musical composer Lionel Bart. Syd Barrett's guitar playing is an unremarked upon source.

The other main feeling that was triggered as I delved backwards was, inevitably, that of an overwhelming nostalgia. There were so many images that sprang up in my mind as I turned the pages, that in the end I decided it was perhaps best to look at this story from my perspective now, to see if there was more sense to be made with hindsight of a remarkable journey that I have had the very good fortune to observe, close up.

As you may recall, it was the mid 70s and everything was grinding to a halt. The scene was stagnant and the air was stale. The Rolling Stones had just played six nights at Earls Court and released one of the worst albums of their career. Led Zeppelin were lost, so were The Who, and, above all, The Faces had broken up for good, leaving no one to wave the flag or represent the working class with our dead-head jobs and suede-head memories. Rod was in Los Angeles, Woody was in The Stones and Ronnie Lane, who had seen the light years previously, was well out of it, in both senses of the word.

The real point was that everybody in rock music had lost their way, big time. It wasn't really surprising. All of the above had been involved in music for so many years that the inevitable had occurred; their creative steam had simply evaporated. Or, to put it another way, in 1976 the Stones released 'Black and Blue', not 'Exile On Maine Street'. And if it had been the other way round, would things have been different?

Probably not because if music is to go forward, it has to reinvent

itself, and the qualities that such steps require can only be located in the energy and idealism of the young. Yet, if talent was thin on the ground, in no way did that interfere with the lavish lifestyle that groups of this nature enjoyed and flaunted big time. All of which laid these bands open to a huge critical mauling. Not for becoming irrelevant to people's lives, but for being so obvious about everything. They all did the same things, all made the same moves. There was no sense of anticipation around, no surprises to look forward to.

And that was London. Can you imagine life in Woking? A small town with a quaint High Street, a mainly dull population and a few shops? Thought not.

The only thing going for this town, if you are a writer of any sort, is that it is a perfect symbol of the class divide in this country, a neat divide between poor and rich. Downtown, there are the rough schools and the sprawling council estates that Paul was raised on. Uptown, there are the golf courses and the huge mansions that the discreet members of the establishment inhabit. This sharp polarity gave Paul enough imagery and ammunition to draw upon in some of his most potent songs.

Yet, drive out of Woking and suddenly you are witness to some of Surrey's finest scenery. Indeed, drive down the High Street, go past Paul's old house in Stanley Road and up on the right are the woods and statue he wrote so vividly about in 'Amongst Butterflies'. Paul played blissfully here as a kid. He spent a lot of his time in the beautiful countryside around Woking and it gave him a contentment rare in one so young. He felt the mystery and the beauty of the world and it inspired and thrilled him to bits. Paul had a memorable childhood. His parents John and Ann loved him to death and instilled an unbreakable self-confidence in him. From his mum's tiny transistor, he heard pop music at its best as it grew up into a wonderful melodic, mystic, innovative and experimental creature. Paul was four years old when The Beatles recorded 'Love me Do', five years old when Macmillan's government fell and the '60s began for real, and eight years old when Geoff Hurst scored his World Cup hat trick. He was transfixed by Motown, by Otis Redding and Stax, The Kinks, Syd Barrett's Pink Floyd or Marriott's Small Faces, and 40 thousand other bands that he would later insert into his own work. But that would come later.

His most important influences, as they still are today, were his parents who passed on to him, amongst other things, physical and mental strength, a sharp tongue, a poetic and sensitive nature, a rigid sense of justice and even a touch of mysticism.

And then came a change. Somewhere, going into his teens, Paul changed from a happy-go-lucky child into a sensitive, introverted and isolated teenager who would spend hours in his bedroom, alone with music. Perhaps it was there that one night the thought of becoming a musician arose in his fertile, imaginative mind. Steve Brookes, Paul's first close friend and with whom he formed The Jam, reported just how eerie it was when at 13, Paul relayed to him one day, in a very matter-of-fact voice, that he was going to be a musician all his life. This was not said with any arrogance. It was said as you would tell someone, I'm going to football tomorrow. *Comme ci, comme ca.*

Paul's house at Stanley Road was a two up, two down with a toilet outside. His mum went out cleaning every day and his dad struggled big time to put food on the table and money in the landlord's pocket. Paul has memories of midnight visits from the police or of his dad returning home from work in a rage because the foreman had done a bunk with the wages. It made for a close-knit unit, the best non Italian family I've ever come across.

And, like a good son of the Mediterranean, Paul never forgot the hard work and tribulations his mum and dad went through, nor his roots. Indeed much of the anger that informs The Jam's work came from his fury at a system which rewarded a person's class and not their talents. It is why he has always been left wing by nature and an honorary, guilty Catholic. When the big money first came in, his first

impulse was to give it away.

The Jam's first gig was as a two-piece at Woking Working Men's Club. Before that, when Paul and Steve were not practising, lifting melodies from The Beatles songbook or tramping the Woking streets barefoot at five in the morning (don't ask), Paul caused havoc at school, experimented with dope, sniffed shoe cleaner, went to the Knaphill disco and fumbled around in girls' blouses.

Then one day his parents ignored a stack of bills in the kitchen and bought him a guitar. From that day on his path was set. The Jam started off as a duo and went up to a five piece with the recruitment of Dave Waller, Bruce Foxton and Rick Buckler; Brookes and Waller left, and soon after news started to spread around town that the group were being looked at by a major record company.

In Woking, we were slightly awed when we heard of EMI's interest. Our local band? Going to make it big? From Woking? Impossible. At this time, The Jam were playing Friday and Saturday night at Michael's, Woking's only after-hours club. On the first floor was a disco. Upstairs, the older members gambled. Generally, we 'youngsters', were not allowed in but one night I managed it. The Jam were playing mainly covers, tackling things like 'Tracks Of My Tears' with great aplomb. I was impressed by their musicianship, if nothing else, but I couldn't see how they were going to be signed. There was not enough original material.

A year later, Paul Weller got on a train and travelled to London, a city he adored. From Waterloo station, he made his way to the Lyceum on the Strand. He was dressed as a Mod. It was the logical move. He had heard The Who's 'My Generation' and discovered the most enduring youth cult ever. Modernism reminded him of his suede-head days. It was a cool, clean and detailed look. Plus the music was ace. Great r'n'b, great pop.

Whilst others doggedly hung on for the big boys of rock to issue a masterpiece, Weller ignored them all and went to some of the irregular local Northern Soul events. He drove a scooter around town with 'Class A Mod' on the back of his parka and played 'My Generation' endlessly on his parent's old radiogram. He didn't know it but tonight was going to be special. Tonight, he would witness one out of the few concerts that the Sex Pistols managed to play in this country.

They came onstage, they sneered, they played amphetamine rock and, most importantly, they played 'Watcha Gonna Do About It' by The Small Faces (although typically Johnny Rotten had changed the lyrics to: "I want you to know that I hate you baby, I want you to know I don't care!"). Weller was speeding off his nut with his mates from Sheerwater and it made perfect sense. He had seen the future and it was his.

Punk gave Weller the framework he needed not only to express himself but to find his own artistic voice. Every major musician since pop immemorial has needed that one musical revelation, that one moment when the world suddenly explodes into shape and a blinding light maps out your path for the foreseeable future. Punk was Paul's. From there, Paul would move on to many other musical styles but it was The Pistols who gave him the first glimpse of what could be done. Like your first lover, he would never forget.

Paul loved Rotten's 'couldn't give a fuck' approach. He loved The Pistols' youthfulness. He saw how his own working-class experiences

could now be made relevant and fitted within his music. He had already heard groups such as Dr Feelgood, whose guitarist Wilko Johnson had formulated a chopping r'n'b edge which also added impetus to Paul's playing, and combining these elements he came into his own.

The next year must have seemed like a blur to The Jam. They went from Michael's to the Greyhound to the Hope and Anchor to a free concert in Soho market to a record deal to a single in the charts and on to rucking with rugby players in Leeds. But by then, in truth, punk was over. Gone, in fact, before any of those groups put out a record.

There is much dismissal of The Jam now by Oxbridge writers in their punk history books. It is because The Jam were not mythical or trendy and therefore impossible to hang 'art' themes on. The Jam were undoubtedly part of punk's Holy Trinity—The Pistols, The Clash and The Jam. Amen. If The Pistols were the focus then The Jam stood to one side, The Clash to the other and that was punk. The Jam certainly weren't like the new art-led schoolsters who came along later. The fact that The Jam wore suits and used '60s references, that they came from Woking and that Paul was so sincere about it all, seems to mean they are not regarded as punk. But as I recall it, punk was about doing your own thing, about making music relevant, about not being predictable. And it was precisely the fact that The Jam did not sport safety pins (the Smiley logo of the day) and because Paul *did* write about life in small town Woking that made them punk.

Paul swallowed the manifesto big time. From punk, he learnt to distrust anything that got in the way of music. Punk gave him a burning hatred of rock mythology and also of stardom, which for a shy 18-year-old who only came to life on stage, was a natural leap to make. To this day, these principles still stand.

It allowed him to give full rein to his distrust of the music business and its falsity and, later, it would also make him turn against the movement that had so inspired him. The famous, 'We'll vote Conservative' statement he made in his very first NME interview was

Andrew Douglas

Derrick D'Souza

born out of a naive stupidity (it also would have come from his mum who to this day preaches old-fashioned Tory virtues of lifting yourself up by hard work), but it was also the statement of someone who has just been denied entry to the club lobbing a fire cracker through its window.

After that, it was down to skill. For many people, watching The Jam playing 'In The City' on Top Of The Pops or 'All Around The World' on the Marc Bolan Show was a real inspiration. To see this 18-year-old kid, jerking around the stage in anger and fury, attacking his guitar like it was his worst nightmare come true, his gruff atonal voice barking out his words of hope and resentment, was a revelation. The music, the image, the attitude, all directly inspired Alan McGhee in Scotland, Noel Gallagher in Manchester, Steve Cradock in Birmingham, Marco Nelson in Reading, and a million more kids.

What The Jam achieved was to take punk into suburbia and connect there with all the younger brothers and sisters of the original punks. And because Paul knew these towns so well, knew how they operated, knew all too well how small-town lives were shaped in the local pub and dole queue, at the disco and the game, the factory and the local park at midnight, he became their town cryer.

Everyone from round these parts instinctively responded to the images and stories that flowed from his active imagination. It was a tradition that Paul had encountered through Ray Davies' work and The Jam would be the last great chroniclers of the 'lite a bite' kids and their mothers' private hells. The only problem was that now everyone looked to The Jam for the answers. And they had none.

What they had was melody, commitment, passion, skill, and a relentless touring and recording schedule that by 1980 had made them a real phenomenon. The day 'Going Underground', went in at number one was the day people started mentioning The Jam in the same breath as The Beatles.

Only, it took some time for the group to get there. In 1978, for 'The Modern World' LP, they were firing blanks. And lots of them. Yet, and another 'Concerto' regret, there is a little bit more to this album than I previously thought. Some people's assertion that this album is one of their favourites, took me back to it and the realisation that I had missed 'Life From A Window' and 'London Girl'. In fact, the album is quite a strange affair, listening to which improves with time. In this book, Paul talks about being caught between punk and mod and hits the nail correctly. There is an awful amount of time wasting here. But when this album gets it right, you understand why some hold this album in regard.

It was, of course, 'All Mod Cons' that put The Jam where they belonged. Paul Weller has always operated best with his back against the wall (see 'Wild Wood') and this album was his most coherent lyrically and musically. It was this album that gave the group their sound, their direction, their identity, everything in fact that you need in life. It also gave them a taster of the huge success that was

Derrick D'Souza

heading their way, a peak of recognition that came to an end when it interfered too much with Paul Weller's brain.

Of course, not everything that the group did was great. Every Jam album has a duff track or two ('Music For The Last Couple', 'Planners Dream', etc.) and not every single was a masterpiece. For me, 'Absolute Beginners' being preferred as an A–side to 'Tales From The Riverbank' was a decision of Graham Taylor proportions.

The production sometimes left the listener imagining what could have been and in this respect a case has to be made that their first album was the closest we ever got to hearing the true essence of The Jam. It is a little-known fact but Weller heard the group in his mind as a garage band, producing brilliant two-minute snap shots of pop adrenalin ('But I'm Different Now,' for example), but success and an increasing sophistication in his writing got in the way. The 'In The City' LP may be the closest Paul ever got to realising the sound in his head.

Still, this aside, for a while, they were the best. They really were and that's because good groups make good records but great groups define their time, which is precisely what Weller did for an enormous number of people. The Jam produced working-class music that spoke directly to their class. Their songs, always highly melodic and shot through with anger, achieved precisely what punk had set out to do. The group had an incredibly strong link with their audience, which was mainly male and working class, because both recognised themselves in each other and because the group never took the piss. It's hard enough coming from below. Weller certainly wasn't going to add to anyone's problems. Both sides gave the other huge respect whilst Weller's wordplay and striking images allied with his class A song writing talent attracted a lot of serious respect.

And Weller always looked cool. He knew his group was the spiritual follow-on to every great mod group and he dressed with the same sharpness and detail that he brought to his songs. The man was always one step ahead in the clothes' stakes whilst his astute choice of covers got a lot of people into Northern Soul, Curtis Mayfield, Small Faces and a lot more cool music.

It couldn't last. Paul is never one to stand still and this artistic restlessness combined with the expectations heaped upon his shoulders finally took over in the summer of 1982. The Jam's last studio album, 'The Gift', was at number one, Paul had just got back from holiday, and he and I went for a drink at the Barley Mow, a West End pub. I told him about some girl problems I was having. He told me that he wanted to split the group. That was 14 years ago and it still ranks as one of the bravest decisions that a musician has made in my lifetime.

Last night, Paul Weller was in Los Angeles with Nat his seven-year-old son, whilst his father, John, mounted the stage to receive Paul's Brit award for Best Male Solo Artist of 1996. Paul's current standing in the scheme of things, as the likes of John Squire, Johnny Marr and Noel Gallagher will enthusiastically testify, has never been higher.

On accepting his award, John Weller said, 'I'm the proudest dad in the world,' and a million of us knew exactly what he meant.

Paolo Hewitt, February, 1996.

A cold winter's night on a Thursday back in 1972: on the stage of a working men's club stand two young people clutching guitars. Both are dressed identically in orange loon pants, black and white shirts and blue and white plimsolls. Between them, they have six songs to play, cover versions from such diverse artists as Donovan, Tom Jones and Chuck Berry.

The songs are played through a small amp placed behind them, that the boys — one fair, the other dark — have plugged their guitars into. When each song is finished, the small audience clap politely, sup their beer and quietly continue their game of cards. Most of the clientele are on name terms with one of the boy's fathers, and so, out of respect to him, they try to look interested.

In front of the boys playing dance two people: the fair haired boy's mother and sister, whilst in the background his father tries to whip up some support, shouting encouraging remarks.

Acknowledging the polite applause that greets each song, the boys finish off their set with an old Chuck Berry number and then begin to pack away their gear. There's no encore, but both boys are flushed with an intangible, nervous energy. The night a moderate success, they later sit in a corner sipping an illicit pint under the knowing eye of the barman, running through the highlights of the set, the pair of them touched by a small streak of self-satisfaction.

Paul Weller and Steve Brookes have just played their first public gig in Woking. And played it well.

1

That year, 1958, Woking, a small town in the heart of Surrey, suffered an unexpected outbreak of polio. Before the medical authorities could successfully bring it under control, two children had died and one child was left with a permanently paralysed arm.

Ann Weller was lucky. 18 years of age, married to John Weller for 11 months, she had just given birth to her first child when she contracted polio of the throat. The date was May 25th, 1958. The birth had been successful, but soon after Ann Weller lapsed into illness, and when the registrar approached her for a name for her first born — the parents hadn't then decided — she gave the first that sprang to mind: John William Weller.

It was only when the family regrouped at their house in Walton Road, with Ann now recovered, that they re-named the child, unofficially, Paul Weller. Two months later the Weller's moved home, this time to a house in Stanley Road just off Woking High Street.

For John Weller Paul's birth was a dream come true. 'To tell you the truth,' he recalls, 'having a boy at that time was something I always wanted. People get married and say they don't care if it's a boy or a girl. Well, I always wanted a boy, even before I met my missus. I always wanted to get married and have a couple of kids. I was dead lucky and I appreciate it.'

Both Paul's parents worked. John as a taxi driver, Ann as a cleaner. Typically working class, neither parent had excelled at school and for the young married couple, with a first child, it was hard to make ends meet.

'We were always poor,' says Ann, 'but we weren't poor like desperate. Money was tight. None of us went without, but we didn't have any money. John always worked so we always had food.'

One thing that both parents were resolved to, though, was that their son should want for nothing. If anything he needed was in their financial reach, he would get it. Failing that they would always give him a secure, loving relationship.

'It's always been that way,' says John Weller. 'When he was a kid we spent so many hours together that I would have thought we would have both been fucked up by now. Father and son or not, even mates can go off each other if they spend too much time together. But evidently it didn't come to that.

'We spent loads of time together, going out through the woods and that. Even when I was on the cabs, I used to take him out with me on jobs. I had him standing behind me and when he had been standing for so long, he could hardly bend his legs.'

Ann Weller took a similar interest in their son's upbringing. 'I can remember taking him to see Elvis Presley in the pictures at Woking Odeon,' she recalls, 'and he had a little blue plastic guitar. He was about five or six, and he used to stand in the aisle and play guitar while Presley was on the screen. Mind you we're all musical, we all love music. We had music on all the time.'

By now Paul had been enrolled at his first school, Maybury Primary, Walton Road and Ann Weller was pregnant again, this time with a daughter, Nicola. Because of the age gap, no real bonds were made between the children.

'What's a five year old got to do with a baby?' Ann Weller reasons. 'Not much have they? When he was 15 and she was ten, he didn't want to know. They didn't quarrel or fight, they just didn't speak. Just hello and that was their lot. At least they weren't fighting. Those five years is quite a lot of difference, especially when you're that young. I mean, now it's nothing. They get on quite well.'

Soon after John Weller quit his taxi job for a place on the building sites where the work was harder but the pay better; it was an essential move to support his growing family. And by the time Nicky was five, Paul had left primary school for his only secondary school, Sheerwater Comprehensive. With him he took his love for a group he had become completely besotted with — The Beatles.

'He was Beatles mad,' remembers Ann Weller. 'Like most kids keep their clothes in their chest of drawers. Paul kept his Beatles records in there and the clothes went where they could. He's got every *Beatle Monthly*. Paul's got the original collection. I went to this rummage sale once and I got a whole box of them, someone was just throwing them out, although some of them he's already got. He used them for cutting up and putting in a scrap book. He had about twelve or thirteen scrap books.'

Weller himself acknowledges his love for John, Paul, George and Ringo and the effect they were to make upon him and his songwriting in later life. 'I used to listen to The Beatles all the time,' says Paul, 'which now sometimes I regret. It is really limiting, but at the same time I also think I learned a lot about songwriting as well. I've got more edge than other people because I understand the songs more. Like, when I write songs I still do it in a quite old fashioned way. I'll have a verse and I'll have a different chorus and I'll have a different middle eight. Stuff like that. I got that from The Beatles thing.'

Another early passion of Paul's was his fanatical interest in clothes. Round about ten or 11, he developed a fashion sense that has never deserted him. 'Around '71 he was into the suede head thing,' his mum explains. 'I mean, people think that Paul sort of went into the mods just to get on. But Paul was a mod at 11. He used to have a good paper round then. He used to have a morning round and he also had the *Evening News* one. He used to save up his money for about six weeks and he'd go off to Petticoat Lane every Sunday when he had enough money.

Paul age 3 1961

Paul and Nanny

'See, Paul was small, he was really small and like in Woking, Dazzles used to have all the mod gear, but nothing would fit Paul because he was too tiny. So we used to have to go up Petticoat Lane because up there you can get it from two year olds onwards. He got his first crombie up Petticoat Lane for 12 quid. Paul has been well dressed, and dressed like he does now, since he was 12.'

But Weller wasn't indulging in the 'mod style', because at that time he was completely unaware of mods, and he was merely following the fashion of the day, a mixture of the skinhead and suedehead influence. They were clothes that a sharp working class kid would do his best to get into. Weller's appearance set him apart at school.

'In the first year he really stood out as being more fashion conscious and a bit sussed than everybody else,' remembers Steve Baker, an old school friend of his. 'Like, he had all the gear. When you're 11 or 12 you're nothing are you? But he was trendy. He had everything. Loafers, Dr Martens, three or four colours of sta-prest, and by the time everyone else caught up he was interested in a different fashion. And then the next one up. He was always one step ahead.'

Despite the flash appearance, Paul Weller was nervous and reserved while at school. He made few friends and the ones he did he stuck to loyally. He had few girlfriends, and as time passed any interest he may have had in the educational system quickly disappeared.

◆

A Christmas present of a guitar from his father finally put the seal on things. For the first year he just left it under his bed, only dragging it out to pose in front of the bedroom mirror and conjure up the images of success that it would bring him. 'Then one day,' says Weller, 'I just decided to really learn it. I had lots of strange ideas about being able to pull birds with it. All really terrible clichés, but they're all fucking true. You sit in the fucking classroom with some old wanker droning on, and just daydream. You see yourself in the local youth club playing and all of a sudden you have this sexual magnetism.'

Once Paul had decided to learn this instrument, his future suddenly became clear. After a year of practice he met up with a new arrival at the school, Steve Brookes. Paul was 13. 'Everything fell into place when I met Steve,' states Paul. 'Before he'd moved down from London and came to Sheerwater, I'd already got really involved with playing the guitar and singing, and all I really needed was to find some other people who felt the same way. So it was like that was the thing that really spurred it along for me, because we just got on immediately and felt the same way about everything.'

Because of troubles Steve was having at home, it wasn't long before he moved in to Paul's house and their relationship became a lot closer. 'We were like, not really brothers, but we did sort of love each other in a way that you can't ever love a girl,' Weller explains. 'We really were close for a time. He more or less lived round our house and he used to share my room. That was probably for a couple of years. Every experience, all the new things we experienced, we were doing together.'

As for school, Weller, with his new found conviction and direction in music, quickly gave up. 'Once I knew for definite what I was going to do, play in a band and that, it was really easy for me because I could just give up. Which I did. I didn't bother any more because it didn't matter. I wasn't worried about books and fucking qualifications or looking for a job. I never had to see the careers officer; I just didn't bother. I didn't need to do any of it. There were a couple of cool teachers who just made a pact with us and said, well, just sit at the back, shut up and don't disrupt and we'll leave you alone.'

The only subjects in which Weller showed any interest were music and English. 'He used to write poetry then,' says Steve Baker. 'Like in English, he'd write an essay and get C+ maybe, if he was lucky. But if he used to write poetry he'd get an A all the time. Poetry he was excellent with, general English average. He never used to talk about books either. Just used to read them on the quiet.'

As Weller divorced himself from the school system, only one teacher, John Avory, the head of music, showed any signs of understanding Paul's feelings. Though Paul says that he didn't learn anything of any musical value from him, it was through Avory that Paul and Steve would perform in the music room during dinner breaks for the other kids. They were their first gigs really.

'There were a couple of other teachers who were not particularly behind me, but just sort of wished me luck,' Weller concedes. 'I remember one time, I don't know what we'd done, but we had to stay in and write these essays. I wrote a really sort of cynical essay about how I didn't want to get a proper job and how that one day I'd look back and sort of gloat on all of them. I actually put all this stuff in and one of the teachers, which was really a surprising reaction for me, said he liked it and wished me luck with it.'

The other consequence of Paul's faith in music as a means of survival, was his separation not only from teachers and education, but from the rest of his peers. Never one to mix socially, because of a strong, insecure streak, it was a dichotomy in Paul's character. His mum, for instance, noting his extreme shyness, couldn't believe that Paul would ever dare to stand on a stage.

'When he said he was going to learn guitar and be on the stage,' she remembers, 'I couldn't see it because Paul is a very reserved sort of person. When he was young he wouldn't speak unless he was spoken to really, not because he was being stand-offish, but I think basically because he's a very shy person. I mean, it takes some guts. It takes some getting used to standing out in front of people and I couldn't believe it when I first saw him up there. Paul was like Jekyll and Hyde to me. Onstage he was a different person because he used to come alive. And then offstage he was back to sitting in the corner with his pint.'

Weller too was aware of this complicated flaw in make up. 'It's really a strange thing,' he says, 'because there's a lot of contradictions. One side of me was really arrogant and knew that I couldn't fail in music, and at the same time I've always had this real self-doubt and lack of confidence. Both those two mixed feelings. It's a weird mixture, but I think a lot of people in music are like that, a lot of them have got that. I think basically, what it is, I was totally confident with music, but I think socially and outside of that, I didn't have the same confidence and arrogance.'

The only people Paul felt any kinship with were those who were musically inclined. Apart from Brookes, he formed a tight knit circle with other school friends like Roger Pilling and Dave Waller, both of whom were learning the guitar. The other kids they sneered at. 'We tended to look down on all of them,' says Paul, 'we always felt a bit more superior to them. I suppose it's just the attitude you get with music, just makes you more cynical because you see the others slaving away and desperately trying to get their CSEs or 'O' levels and we were really, I suppose, smug about it because we just knew for us it didn't fucking matter.

'That's the other thing music does, it separates you, it totally separates you. People say, after you get successful, do you feel detached from real life? But it doesn't even start with being successful, it starts right from the time you make your mind up to get involved in music. It's just a totally different thing. You haven't got the same kind of regularity as everyone else, that mass regularity. And you're experiencing so many different things.'

Though Weller could see, through his friends, where his ultimate destiny lay, he was also developing a strong streak of cynicism, mainly against school and its limitations. But it would extend much further in later years.

'I don't know what it was,' he says. 'I mean, a lot of kids of that age get like that. Steve's really came from the fact that his mum and dad had split up, and I think he had a little bit of a chip on his shoulder about that. I've always been that way really and I don't know why because I've always had a good relationship with my parents. A lot of mine came from school really. Some of it was put on because Steve used to encourage it more, and the rest of it came from school and the way the little system was run. I was really cynical of that. Like tiny, small minds.'

'I think it's also another reason why we never had any other friends outside of our own little crowd. People just used to get fed up with us, we just never took anything seriously. And anyone who tried to speak to us, who wasn't really one of us, we'd just shoot them down in flames really. But me and Brookes had a real strange thing that we really would know what each other was thinking. Someone would be talking to us and we'd look at each other and think this is an idiot, or whatever, that sort of thing. Basically we all understood each other and we had, more or less, the same sort of feelings about things.'

As Steve was spending so much time at Paul's house, it wasn't long before they began writing songs together and improving as musicians. 'They went to this bloke in a music shop in Woking,' Steve Baker remembers, 'and he used to teach them how to play silly songs and scales and all that. Smithy his name was. Regular sort of stuff. Like Paul would play chords and Steve would just strum out a melody. 'Groovy Kind Of Love' and daft songs like that.'

The direction their own songwriting went was in The Beatles mould as Steve shared some of Weller's love for the group. Together they wrote poppy material such as 'Loving By Letters', 'One Hundred Ways To Love You' and 'More and More', every one a love song. Typically, Paul's parents immediately supported his efforts, offering every assistance possible.

'I mean, I'm not really an educated person,' John Weller explains. 'I couldn't put a lot of stock in education because I've never had it. I figured that Paul wasn't a brains trust anyway, none of us were, but he was good at what he was doing so I figured to myself that we should do what we could to enlarge that talent. And I never lost heart in the thing. I thought it would take off. I always had that feeling. I felt he was the right person, given the opportunity, with the kind of songs he was writing and the enthusiasm he had for music, he deserved some sort of push somewhere along the line. I didn't have a £1,000 to put into them, but I had a 1,000 hours, so that's what I did.'

Using his contacts around town, John began hustling gigs for the boys. Pubs, clubs, weddings, anywhere that would accept them. Paul and Steve were playing mainly cover versions with a couple of their own tunes thrown in for good measure, so there were never any complaints.

At school they would play or practise in the dinner hour with Paul regularly phoning up his mum to bring equipment down, just another measure of the support his parents were giving him. 'Paul wanted an amp when he was getting going,' says Ann Weller, 'so we had the phone cut off. If it was a choice between Paul getting a guitar or something or paying the bill, we'd get the guitar. A lot of parents would say, you can't have that and can't have this, whereas John and my attitude was, well, you want it, you got it. If we could afford it. If we couldn't, we'd leave the bill. So I suppose we weren't really good parents in society's eyes, but we've always been like that. A bit harum scarum.'

After a year of playing together, Paul and Steve both decided to expand the line up into a proper group. Pub gigs were okay, but not what the boys were after.

'I remember this one night,' says Ann Weller, 'they played in a

pub and Paul said, what shall I do now dad? We've done all the songs. And he said well, play them again. Least it's passing trade in the pub. Because they were either getting rid of them or else they were just coming in.'

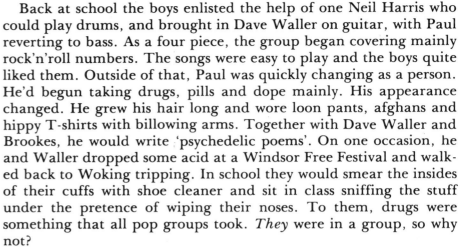

Back at school the boys enlisted the help of one Neil Harris who could play drums, and brought in Dave Waller on guitar, with Paul reverting to bass. As a four piece, the group began covering mainly rock'n'roll numbers. The songs were easy to play and the boys quite liked them. Outside of that, Paul was quickly changing as a person. He'd begun taking drugs, pills and dope mainly. His appearance changed. He grew his hair long and wore loon pants, afghans and hippy T-shirts with billowing arms. Together with Dave Waller and Brookes, he would write 'psychedelic poems'. On one occasion, he and Waller dropped some acid at a Windsor Free Festival and walked back to Woking tripping. In school they would smear the insides of their cuffs with shoe cleaner and sit in class sniffing the stuff under the pretence of wiping their noses. To them, drugs were something that all pop groups took. *They* were in a group, so why not?

'We weren't really peace and love merchants,' explains Weller, 'I think it was more really a drug thing. At that time, if you were in a group, you took drugs, which is really fucking boring when you think about it now. But that's how it was. We thought it was pretty hip doing it. It wasn't so much psychedelic, it was just sort of hip and stoned. Like the whole rock'n'roll thing, I suppose; everything I hate now, but at that age our big dream was to buy a house that we could all live in, if we were ever rich and successsful. Buy a big house and have one room with a great big lump of dope in it burning all day, which we'd go in and smell. Get stoned on. Really dopey fantasies we had. We were always going to buy a barge and live on it; really sort of idealistic things, but in the rock'n'roll tradition.'

Along with the drugs, Paul not only estranged himself further from school, but also from his family, especially his mum. 'I've always got on really well with my mum,' says Paul, 'but there was a period of time, when you go through that adolescent thing, where we just couldn't communicate. I think it was just things like going to the pubs and coming home pissed.'

No undue trouble was caused by Paul's 'rebellious' period, mainly because Ann was still relatively young and could understand what he was going through. 'I'm not that much older than Paul,' she says. 'It's only 18 years which isn't a lot, and I can remember when I was a teenager, whereas a lot of people, when they get older, they forget which is why they don't get on with teenagers.'

As for the group, it now had a name. Nicky, Paul's sister had thought of it. 'We were at breakfast one day,' recalls Ann Weller, 'and Nicky said, well, we've had the Bread, and we've had the Marmalade, so let's have The Jam.'

So The Jam it was. First off, though, it was Paul Weller And The Jam, a fact borne out by the inscription on a cup the boys won in 1973 as best local group.

'What they did,' says Ann, 'was they had to go through a heat in Sheerwater and they won that. Then all the groups from each club went to the old Woking Community Centre for the final.'

One group who were also in the final were Rock Island Line, who had just finished playing a major part as a teddy boy group in the David Essex film, *That'll Be The Day*.

'So Paul, Neil Harris, Dave and Steve turned up,' Ann continues, 'and like Rock Island Line said, you might as well go home all you lot. We'll win this. They thought they were really *the* people. And they didn't win it! Paul won it. It was really great. Funny little thing, but to them it was like winning the World Cup or something.'

Despite the relative success, there were still problems within the band. Neil Harris was also playing with an orchestra as well as The Jam, and it started to disrupt rehearsals Paul had arranged at his house. After the talent show, things came to a head and Harris left.

Practise time, however, was no problem because of where Paul's house was situated. 'Stanley Road,' explains Ann Weller, 'is right on a main road and the traffic was so bad any noise was drowned out. They had to knock it on the head at 9 or 9.30 because of the neighbours, that was when the traffic started to die down. Well, once you stopped having the buses and lorries it became a little bit quieter. But May, next door, she was fantastic. She didn't care a damn. She lived on her own and she used to love it. It used to keep her company and we always said to the neighbours, if it gets too much, you just knock and tell us. End of story. But they had quite a good practise. They used to do it from the time they came home from school.'

With the departure of Harris, the boys already had in mind who they wanted as a replacement: Paul Buckler, a kid who had been two years above Paul at school. 'I think me and Waller had met him one day at a bus stop,' Weller says, 'when we were both stoned and Rick was really straight at the time. He was a bit of a hippy. He had really long hair and listened to Black Sabbath and all this crap which we hated. But really he was very straight. And he was taking the piss out of us cos we were falling about stoned and that. This fucking stuff we used to sniff.

'Anyway, we just asked him because we knew he was a drummer. Asked him if he wanted to come to rehearsal. It's just that in Woking there are no musicians, not our age anyway. So he was the only drummer around.'

The Jam proper had started to take shape.

Michaels Club '74

Paul Richard Buckler was born on December 6th, 1955, five minutes before his twin, Peter. At that time the Buckler family lived in Church Street, Woking. His father was a postman in the sorting office, and his mother stayed at home to look after the family which also included Rick's two older brothers, Andrew and John.

The Buckler parents had always been keen for their children to have the best, and that meant following the traditional route of a good education followed by a secure job.

'We've always been very conscious about their education,' explains Mrs Buckler, 'and it was a big shock for Paul to be in a group. It was something that never entered our heads. See, John is a teacher and Andrew is an accountant, and we've always wanted the best for the boys. We wanted them to have a good education and we let them stay at school till they were nearly 18.'

Paul's childhood was a relatively normal, peaceful one. He attended Goldsworth Primary School and then Sheerwater Comprehensive. In between he was a member of the Boys Brigade and went to Sunday School as the Buckler family — until recently — were regular church goers.

'That was another part of their upbringing,' says Mr Buckler. 'All four boys attended Sunday School. Baptist that is. See, we always went to Sunday School when we were kids, though of course now, once you get to a certain age, about 14 or 15, you drift away from it.'

Both brothers, however, were given piano lessons when young, and they lasted for four years. 'Pete stuck at it,' says Mrs Buckler, 'but Paul... the teacher used to come out and say that Paul is sitting there with his hands behind his back and he won't play! But he could play it by ear, knock things out with one finger.'

'A waste of time to him,' says Mr Buckler, 'with her breathing down his neck when he could get these tunes out, but not in the proper way. And it's a funny thing when you come to think of it, because Pete stuck by it and plays quite well, yet it's Paul who has got on in music.'

The next instrument that Paul — now nicknamed Rick — took an interest in was drums. At school both his brother and another guy called Howard, had decided to form a group: Rick on drums, Pete on bass and Howard as guitarist.

'We never really pushed anything,' Rick says about this first group, formed when he was 15. 'We never had any decent material or anything. It was just something that we were all interested in. All three of us were into music and wanted to do more than just sit around and listen to it.'

The music that caught Rick's imagination at the time was contemporary rock. Heavy metal basically. 'But the fascination for me,' explains Rick, 'wore off when we started playing it. You suddenly realise that it's just boring to play. So that obviously changed my attitude in terms of musical taste.'

Practising mainly around Howard's house, or in the garage of a kindly, local doctor, the band lasted for a year, on and off, never managing to play live. Meanwhile, Rick had done well enough at school, passing the necessary exams, to ensure a place in the sixth year. And unlike Paul Weller, who he knew vaguely, Rick had no real grudges against Sheerwater or the education system in general. Though as he grew older his interest in academic subjects began to diminish.

'I quite enjoyed it really,' Rick says of Sheerwater Comprehensive. 'I mean, most of the people that I knew at school were really good friends. The school itself wasn't bad, even though at the time it had a reputation for being a bit rough. Anyway, by the time I got to the sixth year I hadn't really got any interest in school, 'O' levels and things like that. Even though I went through and did the CSEs and 'O' levels and even started 'A' levels, I was only pointing myself in the direction of the things that I really wanted to do.

'Like, I was interested in woodwork, so I used to spend a lot of time doing that, and I used to bunk off more and more towards the end of the time I was at school. I mean, obviously, my parents, they wanted me with a secure job and with some sort of future. But I got halfway through my first year of 'A' levels and I'd had enough.

'It's a really difficult time for kids at school, because most of their mates are out earning money, and I don't think that situation has changed from when I was at school. You feel like a bit of an idiot really. Well, not an idiot, but left out of things.'

Against his parent's wishes, Rick left school at 17 for a job in a garage. 'I was a bit worried at first,' he recalls, 'because the first job I got was working in a motorbike garage and my parents kept pushing, why don't you go for a respectable job? I went through several jobs and ended up working in a drawing office. I soon found out I didn't really like it, even though that was one of the things at school that I liked doing. When I had to do it for a job I just thought, no, this isn't for me'.

But by then Rick had joined The Jam.

Sheerwater County Secondary School

Name: P. Weller   Report for: Summer Term, 19 71

Teaching Group: 2A3   House: Curie

Conduct: Poor   Group Position: 25   No. in Group: 30

Absent: 15 times.   Late: .... times

Pupils are graded on a five point scale, A. - E,
according to their performance within the teaching group, **not** the whole year group.

Subject	Grade	Exam. Mark	Exam. Pos-tion	Comments	Teacher's Name
English	C	33	27	Could do better if he made up his mind to concentrate and didn't allow himself to be distracted	P. Brown
Mathematics	D	24	27	Must work a great deal harder and pay attention	M. E. Saunton
French	D	36	18	Concentration spasmodic. Must show greater application to work.	G. Hill
Geography	C	64	12	Surprisingly good result	Irving
History	C	44	16=	Paul is capable of a much higher standard	W.
Biology	C	42	15	Inconsistent work.	M. Dufong
Chemistry					
Physics					
General Science	D	16	24	Troublesome and destructive boy.	MJ. Mugford.
R.E.					
Music					
P.E					
Homecraft					
Dress					
Art					
T.D.	C			Progressing slowly	A. Stansford
Metalwork	C			Generally satisfactory.	
Woodwork					
Rural Biology					

HOUSE REPORT: Much more effort needed in all subjects, although his attitude to school, and general co-operation have improved during the year.   M. O. Snider

FORM TUTOR

This report is much worse than it ought to be for a boy of Paul's capabilities. His behaviour in class often leaves much to be desired. His work will not improve until his attitude does.   J. Harrison

HOUSEMASTER/HOUSEMISTRESS

GENERAL COMMENTS

Must do better!   E. Hall.

DEPUTY HEADMISTRESS/SENIOR MASTER

Not a good report but his form tutor's remarks are encouraging. Settle down to work before it is too late.   J. P. Osborne

HEADMASTER

D577

An hour's drive from London, Woking is a town of extreme contrast. All around this small, yet expanding slice of suburbia lie either typical council estates populated by faceless houses, or extremely wealthy areas like Hockering or Hook Heath estates where large houses are lived in by Lords, Ladies and servants. There's the wealth typified by golf courses and large cars, or struggling families whose fathers can be found in the pubs or whose mothers scrub the floors each day. Slowly, Paul Weller was becoming conscious of the environment's contradictions.

'I wasn't aware of class distinctions as such,' he says, 'because when you're mixing with kids at school you don't think of people in terms of race or class. But it was probably just going round friends' houses and seeing how they lived that first made me aware. But at the time class didn't enter into it.

'But I used to knock about with a kid whose parents were a bit posh and lived on this posh estate. I would just get embarrassed if he came round to our house because Stanley Road had an outside shithouse, no bathroom and only a cold tap; y'know, they were Victorian though the house itself was nice because of the way me mum had done it up.'

The Jam, however, were begining to take some kind of direction.

With a standard repertoire of rock'n'roll numbers, they secured a gig, through John, at the Sheerwater Youth Club. 'We set up and were ready to play,' says Steve Brookes, 'and all the gear packed up just before we went on. So we thought, oh sod it! Let's just get pissed. Then somebody went and fixed everything for us and we had to go on absolutely legless. We were falling about and we couldn't play, and John Weller went crazy, because he'd borrowed loads of gear for us and we'd buggered it up.'

Even so, included in their set was an early version of 'Takin' My Love', a Weller song that would eventually show up on The Jam's debut LP.

At the same time the line up was changing. David Waller was asked to leave. 'Just because he was really lazy,' says Weller. 'He never practised and he couldn't really play the guitar anyway and he couldn't sing. We just fell out really. But he accepted it anyway; he knew he wasn't any good on the guitar. We just carried on, the three of us.'

As usual Paul's parents were doing all they could to help their son. For instance, the bass Paul played was a Hoffman, an exact copy of the one Paul's hero Paul McCartney played.

'We went to Kingston one day,' says Ann Weller, 'and we were walking down this little lane and there, in this shop, was this Hoffman bass hanging up. Paul McCartney had a Hoffman bass, so we went in and the bloke in the shop didn't really know what it was. Anyway it was £75. Well, £75 in those days, even though it's not so long ago, was like forget it. But I said, oh we've got to get it for Paul. So what we did was, we swopped him two of his old guitars and I think we gave the bloke about £30 to get it.'

With Waller gone, the trio picked up shows wherever they could. Both Paul and Steve, by now, had dropped their druggy look and reverted back to smarter clothes, both on and off stage. 'That was the other thing,' says Weller, emphasising the closeness he and Steve shared. 'We all used to pick up on things at the same time — and when I say *all*, I suppose I mean me and Steve. We'd kind of do something for a little time then drop it and do something else. Anyway, we smartened up. I suppose we just looked like lads. We started wearing smart clothes, not mod clothes, but smart clothes. Like we cut our hair a bit shorter, just little fads we used to pick up on. It was the same thing with drugs, we wouldn't bother with them after a while. I think everyone does it. I think everyone, in their own little circle, has their own little fads.'

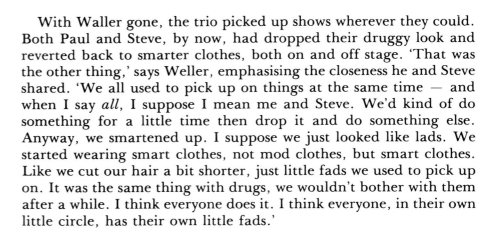

Meanwhile, Paul had reverted back to guitar, but everyone involved realised that a fourth member was required if anything was to become of the band. Even then, however, the group stuck out from all the other local competition. They were the only ones to wear and promote some kind of stage image. The only ones to cover Beatle songs whilst the rest of the opposition churned out Status Quo numbers all night. They had even made demo cassettes of original songs like 'Blueberry Rock' to promote themselves in Woking and elsewhere.

For Weller he had all he needed: purpose in life. School was just an unpleasant diversion for him. 'There was this house master,' recalls Steve Baker, 'and when we were leaving school he was saying, if you get a job you can leave school tomorrow, because at the time there was something of a teacher shortage. And he said, you can't leave school Weller, you got to get a real job. But Paul was like earning £15 a week doing regular gigs so there was no real point in him staying on.'

In fact Weller, in his last year, was spending more time at home, through suspension, than he was at Sheerwater. 'I used to get quite fed up,' says his mum, 'because Osbourne (the Headmaster) down there used to say, can you come and collect him? And I said to him one day, you're not punishing Paul because all you're doing is giving Paul a fortnight off school and he loves it. The only person you're punishing is me because I've got to have him home, trying to find what to do with him. Have you got money for this? And have you got that? Paul would ask me, so he wasn't really punishing Paul. It would have been better if he had given him the cane and wrapped it up at that. And it was stupid things. I mean, when he played hookey they never used to suspend him, and then for running in the corridor or catching him smoking they used to kick him out of school for a fortnight. Bloody daft.'

Paul Weller finally left Sheerwater Comprehensive in 1974. His time was devoted completely to the band, although he would sometimes accompany his dad on a building job. But for the time being he was more interested in finding a new member for The Jam. Although auditions had been held at the top of a pub in Woking, no one suitable turned up. Not until they met up with Bruce Foxton that is.

Born on September 1st, 1955, Bruce comes from a family of three. The family have always lived on the Maybury estate, Woking, and both Bruce's parents worked, his father for the local council, painting and decorating, before moving to Charringtons the coal people, where he would go round houses taking orders. Mrs Foxton had various part time jobs, including one at a sports shop in Woking where one of her workmates was Mrs Buckler.

'Well, they were just ordinary, working class,' says Bruce of his parents. 'They didn't go short, but I always remember my dad getting things on the never-never, all HP stuff. He's still got a few debts now.'

As Sheerwater Junior and Comprehensive schools were just off the Maybury Estate, Bruce went to both, where he neither distinguished nor disgraced himself. His favourite pastimes were football and, later on, technical drawing. 'I was pretty conscientious,' recalls Bruce, 'I wanted to do well. Obviously I'd done better at certain subjects, but still never quite made it.'

It was only in the third year that Bruce Foxton started to gain any real interest in music. 'There was a guy,' he says, 'I can't even remember his surname now, Tony something. He was in the fifth form and he gave guitar lessons, so I thought I'd have a few lessons. I didn't carry on that long because once he showed me a few chords and bits and pieces, I thought I'd pick it up by ear.'

The only music Foxton listened to at home was his elder brother's Motown collection, whilst his own record buying, like Rick's, tended towards the groups of the day: Bad Company, bands like that.

At school Bruce passed a few CSEs and left not really knowing what he wanted to do. His parents, again like Rick's, wanted a steady job for him, and in 1971, the year he left school, Bruce became an apprentice compositor in the print trade.

'I didn't really get much help from the careers officer,' he recalls, 'and it was like, oh well Derek, my brother, he's a compositor. It seemed a pretty good job, good money at that time, and so I thought I might as well have a go at it.'

After a couple of years, Bruce met up with a couple of guys at work who wanted to form a group. Zita they called it, and Bruce joined as a guitarist. As the pair of them lived 15 miles away in Godalming, Bruce would travel over there and rehearse. 'It was just heavy rock,' says Foxton. 'They wrote their own stuff, but we didn't get past the stage of rehearsing. Going over to Godalming, rehearsing and not getting anywhere.'

Whilst with Zita, Bruce also attended another audition round the bedroom of a guy who lived in Woking. The material was completely different, Beatles stuff mainly, and the two guys Bruce met impressed him with their musicianship and vocal abilities. He had one rehearsal and went back to Zita in two minds about whether he should join them or not. He decided against it.

Steve Brookes at Michaels Club '74

Two years later he met Paul Weller and Steve Brookes again. This time he had no qualms in taking up their offer and joining The Jam as a rhythm guitarist. 'Well, I just wanted to play live in front of people at the time,' recalls Foxton, 'and I was getting really frustrated. It was all rehearsals, rehearsals, but it just didn't seem to get anywhere. When I heard the stuff Steve and Paul were playing, at least it meant we could get some gigs. I thought we had more of a chance of doing it with the stuff Paul and the guys were playing, as opposed to heavy metal and trying to get the odd college date here and there.'

Bruce Foxton had made the right choice in shelving Zita.

Just by chance, Paul Weller heard a song called 'My Generation' by The Who on a tacky K-Tel compilation album, and it changed his whole way of thinking. He became a mod. Backtracking to the '60s, Weller found out all he could about all aspects of modernism, especially the clothes and music. To Weller it was the identity he'd unconsciously been searching for.

'It made me feel separate and kind of individual,' remarks Weller. 'It also gave me a direction, something to base myself on. I think at that time there was just nothing at all, nothing to be a part of. So it was like a base to work from. It gave you a sense of purpose, and I think the fact that I was totally isolated and the only person into it was even more encouraging.'

Soon Paul had acquired a scooter and covered it with mirrors and stickers, fur seat and all. Never one to get excited about contemporary music — apart from Dr Feelgood — his record collection became mainly '60s — Motown, Stax, The Who, anyone who the original mods had latched onto.

'I used to work like 100 yards down the road,' remembers Steve Baker, 'and one day he came into work with a parka on and said, can you do a job for us? He was on a scooter wanting some holes put in it so he could have more mirrors. And on the back of this parka, he had this big circle, and written in chalk he had 'Mod Class A'. He said, I'm really into mods. I heard a Who LP the other day, it's brilliant; 'My Generation', I love it. He used to listen to all this '60s stuff, The Kinks, The Who, Beatles of course, Small Faces, and he used to have all the gear. He was always going to get a mod revival going.'

'Discovering the mod thing also struck some kind of chord with my memory,' Paul explains, 'I had been a suedehead — or smoothies, as they were known — and a lot of the suedehead clothes and culture were obviously a direct follow-on from the mods: the association with black music and dancing, the Ivy League shops, Royal's shoes, Sta-prest, Ben Shermans and Brutus shirts. So it was recapturing that mentality which was exciting for me.'

Obviously Weller's new found interest was to be reflected in the group. Gradually they dropped their rock'n'roll covers in favour of soul songs, such as 'Heard It Through The Grapevine', and Weller began writing in a '60s vein.

Within the group, however, tensions were developing. Although Rick had proved a competent drummer, Weller always found himself arguing with him. 'He used to be really awkward,' says Paul. 'He just got a bit dangerous, started chucking things around. I always have this picture of him being really fucking awkward. He's really quiet now, but before he used to be really fucking mad. It must be something in drummers, a little bit like Keith Moon.'

Rick himself remembers his early character. 'Stupid things I used to do,' he says. 'Like not talking for a day or smashing up somebody's guitar and hitting people on the head with mike stands. Getting drunk all the time. I suppose it's the things that you do anyway, kids I mean, so my actions were no more extrovert than anybody else's.'

Another problem was Steve Brookes' dislike of Bruce. Nothing had been said, but both felt the animosity. Also the close partnership of Brookes and Weller was slowly falling apart. 'For instance, when I left school,' says Weller, 'I never worked for two years, never done anything at all. Just used to play all day long. And Steve was the same way for a while, but then his mum moved down to Woking with him and his brother, and he had to go out to work; she needed the dough.

'So that separated us a bit because you start to go through different experiences, you don't follow the same experience. Also he met this bird and was really involved with her. I used to get really jealous of that. It was like she took him away so that really split us up.'

Also Weller's mod infatuation was something that Steve Brookes couldn't relate to or take seriously. The problem was compounded by Weller's inablility to get on successfully with Bruce and Rick. 'I never used to speak to any of them,' Weller says. 'I would try to avoid speaking to them. I just really hated them. This was prior to Steve leaving, we just failed to communicate.'

It took all of John Weller's ingenuity to keep the group going, keep them apart from each other and yet still interested in playing. Because slowly but surely, gigs from further afield were starting to come in. John had already managed to secure them a Friday night residency at Michaels, a local club, with the owner allowing them to rehearse on Wednesday nights.

'Besides that,' says John, 'we were doing weddings, 21sts, anything, and we were getting £30 a night or whatever it was. We even played Chelsea FC because I knew Harry Medhurst, the trainer. And for the Chelsea show we got £100. Magic price.'

By now Paul had reverted to rhythm guitar and Bruce, who couldn't quite cut it, had started to learn bass. With the money the band earned from their regular shows, more equipment was bought and one night, after a show in Hindhead, a woman who worked there arranged an audition for the group with her boss Terry Slater, an A&R man at EMI.

'We set up an afternoon session especially for him,' says John Weller, 'with the group playing the numbers they had written themselves. He said he'd let them know. He gave them a pass really; nicely, but he gave them a pass.'

To get anywhere, John Weller knew he would have to start getting the group London dates. As a teenager John had done a lot of boxing and from those boxing days he knew a guy called Duncan Ferguson who ran the Greyhound pub in Fulham Palace Road. John, using all his blagging technique, finally badgered Ferguson into giving The Jam a chance. They were given support slots to Thin Lizzy and Stackeridge.

'At the Stackeridge one,' recalls Ann Weller, 'they had all turnips thrown at them. Stackeridge came from Dorset, or somewhere down there, and all their supporters used to bring turnips, because it was turnip country, and throw them.'

With Bruce still not that confident on bass, The Jam would play as a trio and bring Bruce on for the last four numbers. It was after one of these Greyhound shows that Steve Brookes finally decided that the group's direction — which Paul, through his mod interest, was steering them — wasn't for him. He quit.

'I think he was a little bit fucked up,' says Weller. 'Things with his family, things with his girlfriend, just generally a bit fucked up about things. It really just came to a head. He didn't particularly get on with Bruce either, so he left. It was a mutual thing really.'

With the departure of Brookes, The Jam placed ads looking for a keyboard player to complement their evolving sound. No one could be found, so the group settled down as a trio. 'I think it just kind of fell into place,' says Weller. 'There was less friction in a way; the group balanced itself a little bit more. It's always been a little bit divided I think, probably not so much in recent years.'

Having Paul's father as a manager was something that could have caused problems; of which John Weller was well aware. 'I've never had the slightest inkling of anybody saying anything,' he says, 'because even in those days there was no favouratism. I never favoured anybody purposely; I probably used to go too much the other way if anything.'

By all accounts there was only one nasty incident that marred these formative days. One night, after a gig at Michaels, both Bruce and Rick were convinced that John and Paul had done them out of some money. They both quit, after an argument. A week later they were back together again.

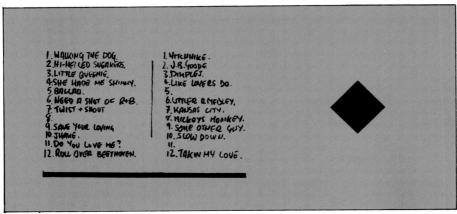

An early set list (74'ish) at
The Greyhound

'Rick and Bruce have never levelled the criticism that my dad was one sided,' says Paul, ''cos I think he's always been fair. We've never had that trouble, it's never existed. I think I've probably mellowed out as well. I could be a real cunt. I should imagine I could be quite awkward to work with as well, my different temperaments and that. It's a really difficult thing to get all the people's personalities to blend in a group, really fucking difficult. Most difficult thing was to even find people in the first place. But to actually get on... I'm amazed that we did manage to stay together. because we hated each other so much then, it's incredible.'

Through the shows the band were getting at the Greyhound, John Weller started taking tapes of the group around record companies, sacrificing precious time off work. 'Decca, Pye... you name it, I went there,' he says. 'I used to borrow money off Ann, a fiver out of the housekeeping. We had this old Austin that used to do about 40 miles to the gallon, put a quid in and you had a bit of petrol. A couple of quid used to get me up to London on a Wednesday or a Thursday. I used to phone them up prior to that, but I never got any joy. So I thought fuck this, and I went and saw them.'

Meanwhile, Paul had stumbled on a group who he found inspirational: Dr Feelgood. 'The Feelgoods,' he says, 'that was another big influence, one that was never really mentioned before. I remember seeing them on a Saturday morning show doing 'Back In The Night'. Our style developed from that. Just a bit more R&B and I used to nick a lot of Wilko's stuff, the guitar things. He was like the first sort of guitarist who really made an impression on me.'

Along with Townshend of course, who had by now replaced The Beatles as Paul's main source of inspiration. 'Yeah, definitely,' says Paul. 'I mean, I've always tried to play it down for obvious reasons, but in the early days definitely. I didn't even remember The Who, I didn't know any of their songs, just literally picked up on it in the space of a couple of months. I just copied the sounds from the records and I heard people telling me about what he used to do onstage, the jumps and the windmills. I'd seen an old photo in a magazine and I'd copy the stance or something.'

From these two influences, Weller began pushing his own material in that direction. Songs such as 'I Got By In Time' and 'Non Stop Dancing' were all written in this period, with Bruce and Rick happy enough to accept Weller's new material.

Not that they were having a particularly easy time. Both of them still had jobs to hold down and as the gigs in London increased, so it began interfering with their work.

'We used to start work really early,' says Bruce, 'about 7.30 and when we started getting on the London pub circuit we were getting home pretty late and then having to get up. Obviously you couldn't give your best the next day at work, and that started to show. Then we had to start asking for time off, both Rick and myself, knock off early, and that got really difficult. I don't think they'd have stood it much longer.'

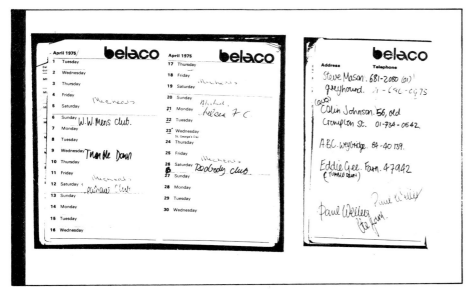

Paul's 1975 diary

Rick's parents especially became distraught at their son's increasingly erratic time keeping. 'Well, I must admit,' says Mrs Buckler, 'that was the only thing that we ever had any argument over. You see, they stayed out late at night which was completely foreign to us. I mean, he never came home till very, very late, then sometimes he'd be at work and Mr Weller would be standing there waiting for him to go to a gig — and he hadn't come home from work. It used to irritate us a bit at the time because we didn't understand.'

The Bucklers weren't too impressed, either, when they went to see their son play. 'I remember going to see them in New Haw,' says Mrs Buckler. 'And I remember that very well because I was in my church coat, my best coat and white gloves, white handbag and feeling very smart. We went over there and it was very, very noisy. You couldn't hear yourself speak. We went up to the bar and there was beer sploshing all over and there was nowhere to sit because it was all messy and horrible. It was disgusting.'

In direct contrast, Weller's mother would be at every show, cheering her son on with Nicky, getting people to dance along with the group and supporting them all the way. Her son, however, was starting to get frustrated at the lack of real success coming his way. 'Mainly we were just playing these clubs,' Paul Weller says, 'and awful working men's clubs, which is like really good money. We used to make a tenner a night each, which was a lot of fucking dough then. We used to play them every weekend. We'd maybe play Friday Saturday and Sunday some weeks. We just seemed to play them for fucking years, but all of a sudden we just started to cut it down. The more gigs we got in London, the more we wanted to cut down on these crappy clubs. We had less money, but it meant we kept it a little more pure. We didn't have to do all these shitty songs.'

What was also happening was that as a trio the band were becoming much closer. Even though there were plenty of rows about the smallest of things — like humping gear in — there were as many laughs, with the three of them happily socialising together in a local pub or getting pissed at a working men's club gig. What held them together, through the fights and depressing times, was their collective belief in The Jam.

'Most of them were over silly things,' says Rick about the fights. 'Just personal disagreements. If you spend three or four hours in a van all sitting on top of the equipment, if something breaks out in the back it's mayhem. You get in the van unscathed and come out with a black eye and you don't know who gave it to you.

'But really that was a good thing. We were all young, full of life and it was probably the force behind us anyway because we all had the same thing in mind. All these frustrating things would happen, like the van would break down and I sat on Paul's bass guitar once and broke the neck off. But we got over it because, basically, that was the thing that was holding us together, the group.'

John Weller was another guiding influence, doing all he could to keep the band alive. When a gig some distance away came up, he would borrow a van from somewhere, rush around scrounging equipment and do his utmost to make sure the band played it. And although the club gigs paid for themselves, once they began in London the money quickly dried up.

'The London gigs weren't really paying,' recalls Rick. 'Like you wouldn't get hardly anything at all. Not enough to pay expenses and drive all the way up to London and back. Plus I was taking more and more time off work because I was going to bed late, getting up late and then going into work at about three in the afternoon, dodging from job to job to stop myself from getting the sack. So John was a great help. It was somebody we could fall back on to. Really, John was like the backbone of the thing right from the word go.'

In 1976 the Weller family moved from their house in Stanley Road to Balmoral Drive on the Maybury Estate. Further up the road in London, things were also changing. By dint of their Greyhound gigs, The Jam had flirted on the outskirts of the pub-rock scene — a circuit that bands such as The Feelgoods and Ian Dury, with Kilburn And The Highroads, were to use as a stepping stone to greater things.

Pub-rock bands were basically an unconscious reaction to the much bigger groups of the day who you could only see in giant arenas. With the arrival of The Sex Pistols in the summer of 1976 everything fell into place. The Pistols weren't a bunch of good time musicians content to churn out 12-bar blues in a dingy London pub. They stood for youth and a brand new attitude which would galvanise kids into action.

Paul Weller was one of those people. Already sick of Woking and the small minds he felt around him, he'd become besotted with London as *the* place to live and work in. When he saw the Pistols, the opening of clubs such as the Roxy and 100 Club to cater for the growing punk movement, when he read about The Clash and what they stood for, when he felt the wind of change which was beginning to sweep London, he knew he *had* to be a part of it all. No doubt about it.

Walt Davidson

'It was so exciting,' he says. 'It's really hard to describe that kind of excitement because it was so fast. It was just really moving. That's how it seemed. Also people forget the fact that we didn't come from London. So while you had all these groups singing about how boring it is in London, for us it was like something else. London was such an exciting place because that's where it was all happening. It certainly seemed that way to me.

One of Paul's neighbours at the time was Steve Carver who Paul struck up a friendship with. Paul already knew his brother Pete from school, but Steve quickly got to know him.

'He used to love London,' recalls Steve. 'I remember he used to say, I'm going up to London with a tape recorder. I'd say what for? And he'd say, I want to *tape* London. I think he idolised it you know. He always thought of it as magical.'

As punk began to spread, so The Jam totally devoted their time to gaining regular London gigs. Consequently, Weller began changing the set away from their soul material, to harder, faster songs, gaining inspiration from bands that he saw, like The Clash and the Pistols.

Nevertheless, Bruce and Rick still harboured doubts. 'I don't think they were quite as involved in it as I was,' comments Weller. 'Not at the early stages anyway. I think afterwards they were. Because there's three years age difference as well; like, I was only 17 so I think that made a difference. I'm the sort of person that if there is something I really believe in, once I really get into it, I don't care about anything else. I just go for it. Whereas with Rick and Bruce they're probably a bit more hesitant about things.

'For a start Bruce still had his job, which is fair enough in some ways, but he wasn't really willing to give it up just like that. Whereas I would never even consider working. It wouldn't make what I was going for as strong. I can't explain it, but if I see something, like a goal, I totally disregard everything else and just go for that. I would never hedge my bets. I've never believed in that.'

However much the future started to look promising for The Jam, money, lack of it, was still a hassle. In fact Paul, still loath to work, sometimes found himself helping out his father. 'One day me and Paul,' says his father, 'had a right fucking barney — I forget what about — he shot off and walked home from Horsley back to Woking. He fucked off and I carried on working. Then I thought bollocks to this after about an hour, but before I left there was a call for me. It was the bloke from the Golden Lion, Sean, and he said, you little wankers have been after me for a job. Can you do tonight? I said sure, but I didn't have a clue where everybody was.

'So I got in my car and shot off to find Paul. As I got about two miles from the site there he was coming back on his little scooter. I flagged him down and told him the news and he said fucking great! We dumped his scooter at home, got in my blue Zephyr and went to get Rick and Bruce. Borrowed this van off a geezer, went round and blagged a lot of gear from different people — all in the space of three hours because we had to be there by seven. We got there about 7.10, set up and played a storming set, cracking night, lots of people there who liked it.

'Then,' he continues, 'we took a job at the Hope and Anchor. We all turn up and who should be there but The 101'ers. I'm arguing with this geezer from the Hope saying you fucking booked us. Anyway made me look a right cunt cos we had loaded all our gear in and we had to take it all out again. Everyone was choked, but the guy said, if you let up tonight, I'll give you a job next week.

'When we did finally play there, there were eight people: Nicky, Ann, Pete Carver and some others. Following time we got the Hope, the guy phoned up and I said, not with eight people. He said give it a go and so we went up. There was tension at the time because the band didn't know anything about there being two other bands on the bill. The other band was pulling them in at the time and we were like support. It just turns out that they didn't show up. It was great, there were about 150 people down there. Of course the following time we played there, you couldn't get down the steps.'

Punk spread dramatically across London, and The Jam quickly became a part of the scene. Not only did it change Weller's songwriting, but his attitude too. The Clash, with their abrasive statements had a particular impact. 'I mean the Pistols didn't have many ideals did they?' says Weller. 'It was just enough for them to exist. But I was really influenced by a lot of things that Strummer said. What they said in interviews was so different, no group had ever fucking said it before. They just showed up the music business for what it was, you know, the whole system. The whole separation of stars and their audience. I had never thought of those things before. Just totally influenced me.'

The emergence of punk didn't mean, however, that Weller would forsake his mod inspiration. What separated the band, for instance, from many of their punk contemporaries, were the black mohair suits they'd begun wearing on their early dates at the Greyhound and still stuck to defiantly. Weller was always suprised that they were accepted in these clothes, but the songs that he was writing were proof enough of his credibility; 'In The City' for instance. 'I had the title for months,' he explains. 'First it was called 'In The City There's A Thousand Things I Want To Say To You', because even then I was into pretentious titles. I used to sing that line to my mates and they would get excited about it even at that stage. I knew it was a classic even before I wrote it because I could see the whole song. All I needed was the riff to go with it, which eventually came. During the early days we would open with it, close with it and encore with it. It was such a powerful song, I don't think the recorded version really ever caught it; it was always different live. I used to announce it as the full, original title, but shortened it because some thought it was over the top.'

So proud was Paul of 'In The City' that he even made up his own badge with the original title of the song written on it, and proudly wore it up the pub on a Friday night. With friends like Dave Waller, Tony Pilot, Pete and Steve Carver in tow, the gang of them would go out on a Friday night, sit in pubs and rip up their clothes, find themselves banned for drunken behaviour, walk into Kentucky Fried Chicken shops and piss against the counters waiting for their food.

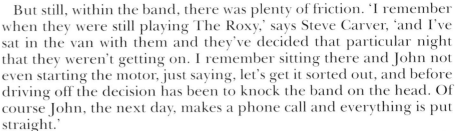

But still, within the band, there was plenty of friction. 'I remember when they were still playing The Roxy,' says Steve Carver, 'and I've sat in the van with them and they've decided that particular night that they weren't getting on. I remember sitting there and John not even starting the motor, just saying, let's get it sorted out, and before driving off the decision has been to knock the band on the head. Of course John, the next day, makes a phone call and everything is put straight.'

Many a time, simply through constant bickering, the group nearly fell apart with Bruce, Rick and Paul going for each other's heads. 'I can remember one argument at the Hope and Anchor,' recalls Foxton, 'when it came to blows between me and Paul, and me getting a black eye. I thought, that's got to be the end of the band. John was freaking. I can't remember what it was over; it could have been anything like loading the gear in or something.'

The group knew though, that their time was approaching. Weller especially. Intoxicated by the London punk scene, there was no way he was going to let go. 'We were meeting new people, and totally different people to people I'd known before. I suppose they were like punks; they weren't like these fucking Pallitoy punks you get today. They looked different, felt different, talked different, and all of a sudden we began to notice the same face at different gigs. It may be like five people you'd see at the same gig. Like Shane, (who later went on to sing with The Nips), was one of them, Adrian Thrills (whose first three copies of his fanzine 48 Thrills carried covers of The Jam before he split for a writer's job on New Musical Express), and this other geezer called Claudio. To see these people who were like fans in a way, the whole thing was so exciting. I loved every minute of it and we just knew that something was really happening and that we were going to happen.'

Walt Davidson

Erica Echenburg

PAUL WELLER

THE JAM SIGN TO POLYDOR

POLYDOR climb aboard the new-wave band wagon, with the signing of three-piece band The Jam. The deal covers four years, and the first release in a few week's time will be the single "In The City". The trio — who consist of Paul Weller (lead guitar and vocals), Rick Buckler (drums and backing vocals) and Bruce Foxton (bass) — are also set for the following dates:

Leighton Buzzard Hunt Hotel (this Saturday), **London Putney** Railway Hotel (March 1), **London Hammersmith** Red Cow (2, 9, 16, 23, and 30), **Leicester** Polytechnic (5), **Canterbury** Kent University (11), **London Islington** Hope & Anchor (18), **London Stoke Newington** Rochester Castle (24 and 31) and **London Royal** College of Art (25)

The Jam
Soho Market

WITH BANDS far exceeding the number of London clubs, sometimes you *really* have to take it to the streets.

Last Saturday, the Jam did just that. Setting up on the pavement outside Soho Market about 12.30, they ripped it up for almost an hour. A small, appreciative crowd developed, complete with beggar. The firemen at the nearby station watched from the roof. The Clash enjoyed their breakfast to the rocking strains.

Natives of deepest Surrey, the Jam looked as though they just released from school, though their black suit-white shirt-black tie combination could be to invoke mid-Sixties Beat Boom correctness. Guitarist Paul Weller must be the quietest guitarist in rock, quite Wilko Johnson influenced, but capable of providing some real excitement. The rhythm section (Ricky Butler — drums, Bruce Foxton — bass) was solid, but could use less cabaret.

Their songs also invoke mid-Sixties Beat Boom, and could do with a bit more musical originality. There're some good things in there, especially 'In The City I've A Thousand Things To Tell You'.

The sun shone, no police came by, and the last three songs were hot stuff. Judge for yourself November 9 at the 100 Club.
JONH INGHAM

23rd October 1976

By now The Jam had started to attract press attention, and when they played a Saturday morning gig in Soho Market, with The Clash watching, they received their first reviews. One of these was from Caroline Coon in the Melody Maker who accused them of being 'revivalists', noting Weller's Townshend-influenced guitar playing. When the review appeared, Weller cut it out, stuck it on a bit of cardboard and wrote underneath it, 'How can I be a fucking revivalist when I'm only 18?'. He then tied it round his neck and wore it to the pub that night. Strange cat.

Revivalist or not, The Jam had now secured a residency at the Red Cow and the Nashville, playing to packed, enthusiastic audiences every time. 'Then Chris Parry (Polydor A&R man at the time) turned up on the scene,' recalls John Weller, 'and took quite an interest. He finally came to the Nashville Rooms one night when it was packed with about 500 people, and he was kind of knocked out by that. So he said about doing a demo. The first Saturday we had the demo arranged we couldn't make it because the IRA had just bombed some part of Oxford Street and it was closed; so nobody could get to Polydor or anywhere else. Then we had to wait about two weeks, and that two weeks seemed like an eternity.

'Parry had just been let down by The Clash at the time. He'd also been let down by the Pistols, who he was after. So he didn't want to let this one go and I had no intention of letting him go, so that was that.

The very first photo-session
after being signed

'But in those days, I couldn't afford to pay the phone bill and so the fucking thing was switched off. He was trying to get in touch with me and the only way he could do that was at the building site I worked at, down in Ash Vale. I told him the house number I was working at and that's how he got in touch. He said, you got to have your phone on, and I said, I ain't got the fucking money. I used to call him from a phone box in Ash Vale, but in the end I thought fuck this I'll give you the number of the house. So I'd be working away and the woman who we worked for, Caroline, used to say, there's a call for you John. Anyway he took us for the demo and signed us up.'

Another press shot. Note the
mis-spelling of Rick's name.

PAUL WELLER

RICK BUCKLEY

BRUCE FOXTON

THE JAM

IN THE MODERN WORLD
A NEW AND EXCITING
YOUNG FANZINE FROM
LONDON.   12P

INSIDE:—AN ACE INTERVIEW
WITH PAUL WELLER OF THE
JAM AND MORE STUFF TOO.

Polydor signed The Jam for £6,000, something that Weller felt a little ashamed about at the time. 'That was something I always used to be really embarrassed about, which is a bit stupid if you think about it, because The Clash signed for 120 grand and the Pistols signed for 40 million or whatever, so I was a bit embarrassed because it was almost like a credibility thing, you know.'

Conversely, Steve Carver can clearly remember Weller's aloof attitude when the news of the signing came through. 'Me and Pete, my brother, were in the Princess pub (Weller's local) with Paul, and Bruce came bouncing in with John and said, we've cracked it. We've got the contract. Paul didn't register at all, and I said to him at a later date that he didn't seem over the moon. To be quite honest, he said, I'd just found my old Who badge in the back of one of my drawers and I was more chuffed about that.'

Rick Buckler's parents were similarly cool when they heard the news. In classic, parental style they asked him when he was going to get a proper job. If at all. Bruce's parents felt the same way, but Bruce had by now finished his apprenticeship, and with that under his belt, matters cooled somewhat.

For the Wellers , though, it was the culmination of everything they'd worked for since Paul was 14. Every sacrifice they'd made, all the hassles they'd gone through together, had now started to pay off. Plus their son's songwriting ability was starting to grow in stature. Evidence of this was a new song Paul had come up with called 'Away From The Numbers'.

'That was another song,' he says, 'that I had the idea for months. I kept seeing it in my head, and even now I still do that. Half the excitement in songwriting for me is what I'm *going* to write. The elusive classic which you always might come up with.

'Anyway, 'Away' was supposed to be a surfing type song, a bit Beach Boys, hence the chorus 'ooos' and 'ahhhs'. It's a very 'mod' song, if you see what I mean. I wrote this over Xmas when I stopped going out and stayed in to feel sorry for myself. It also took me months, about six, to finish, actually finish it. 'Sounds From The Street' was also meant to be a surf song, but we didn't have the vocals to bring it off though.

Paul Weller was 18 and about to embark on a career that would take The Jam, in England at least, to the very top of the tree. All the time he already knew that he was going to make it, which is why he'd sacrificed everything — school and social life — to get there. When, as a fresh faced 14 year old who shy, nervous and withdrawn, he first began to take the guitar *and* his ability seriously, he made himself a promise: 'Which was,' Paul Weller reveals, 'if I hadn't made it by the time I was 20 I'd give up and go and do something else. That's why I was really pleased because I was 18 and making records. You see, I've always had this thing about youth, this thing about ageing.'

It was to be the first of many promises that Weller would make to himself.

A week after signing with Polydor, John Weller received a telegram from Terry Slater, the EMI scout who had looked at the band in 1975. The message, referring to The Jam's first recording contract, read 'that was a bit quick wasn't it?' But by then it was too late.

The group had their first single, 'In The City' c/w 'Takin' My Love', ready for release. A near-perfect summary of what The Jam stood for in both lyrical and musical terms, 'City' was a tough, energetic song skilfully built round a memorable guitar line.

A tribute to London and youth, it immediately gave powerful notice of Paul Weller's songwriting ability, standing proudly apart from the rush of punk singles being released simply because of its intelligent construction. Where others forsook composition for energy (a very fashionable commodity then) Weller's penchant for classic pop composers — Pete Townshend, Steve Marriott, John Lennon, Ray Davies — saw that 'City' was moulded in the pop tradition.

In some circles, however, its lyrical content was completely misunderstood.

"In The City' was always misinterpreted,' Weller recalls. 'A lot of people thought that on that song I was singing, *I'm a city kid* or something, which I wasn't. If you read the lyrics it has got nothing to do with that at all. It was just the feeling of being in London, so it was like a homage thing to London and the scene — the whole punk scene.'

Written a year before, Paul's attitude to the expanding punk movement had by now radically changed. Whereas he had been dramatically fired by its idealism, inspired by the youthfulness of it all (always an important factor for Weller, even today) he was now sorely disappointed by what he saw as the fraudulent behaviour of punk's major groups.

Groups like The Clash, who totally influenced his way of thinking, far from offering a true alternative to rock's hierarchy were actually becoming *part* of it in Weller's eyes.

Not only that, Weller was also experiencing a backlash of inverted snobbery against the group, especially from hardcore punks. Their suits, the fact the group could actually play, Weller's modernist stance and naive political ideology all received critical sneers. *Sniffing Glue, the* punk fanzine, was just one example accusing The Jam of being tighter than the 'London Symphony Orchestra' in one issue. Weller retaliated one night by burning a copy onstage at the 100 Club.

'This is your fucking bible,' he told an uncomprehending crowd, whose dogmatic attitudes Weller detested so much. Things finally came to a head in the band's first *NME* feature.

'All this change-the-world thing is becoming a bit too trendy,' Weller informed writer Steve Clark. 'We'll be voting Conservative at the next election.' Further on in the article Weller calls the Queen, 'the best diplomat we've got. She works harder than what you or I do or the rest of the country.'

Given that The Jam were still sporting Union Jacks on their amps and badges, it was no wonder that punk's 'revolutionary elite' should throw up its arms in pure disgust at such pro-establishment views. According to Weller this was exactly what he'd planned.

'That was really fucking stupid', he says of his pro Conservatives statement. 'But I think it was obvious that this particular little breed would never really accept us. In the end it just pissed me off and I thought, well, fuck you then.

'They really started to get petty about it. *Sniffing Glue* was like the worst for that sort of thing. Also it was because we didn't come from the city as well; we didn't come from London so the little hierarchy didn't like us.'

Such were the attacks on him that Weller retorted by inserting a lyrical snipe at his detractors in 'Sounds From The Street'.

I know I come from Woking / And you say I'm a fraud / But my heart is in the street where it belongs,' he snaps out. And later on, more implicitly, he sings, *'We're never gonna change a thing / And the situation's rapidly decreasing / But what can I do except try to be true? / That's more than* you, *at least I'm doing something...*

With hindsight it's easy for Weller to justify himself and his political stance as simply a wind-up against punk's main core. But certain factors need to be taken into consideration.

At 18 years of age his political overview was hardly wide-ranging. Where people like Strummer, or even Hugh Cornwell, at least had a working knowledge of figures such as Marx or Lenin, Weller was yet to familiarise himself with their philosophies. Not suprisingly George Orwell was the only writer Weller seems to have gravitated towards.

Like Orwell, author of such classics as *1984* or *Animal Farm*, Weller was something of a patriot; not in the right wing sense of scum like the National Front, but one who loved England and naturally wanted to see the best for it. What he saw was rising unemployment, people boxed-up in impersonal council blocks and, worst of all, a small group of rich, powerful people controlling other people's lives through education, work and leisure.

SINGLES OF THE WEEK
THE JAM: In The City (Polydor). First release from the New Wave's finest band, The Jam, and the title cut from their soon-to-be-released album, "In The City" is the most convincing British-penned teenage anthem I've heard in a Very Long Time — perhaps since the halcyon days of the 60s. The song shows The Jam to have been influenced by The Who, and the Townshendesque power chords Paul Weller wrenches from his Rickenbacker back up the impression. But that's like saying the Beatles were influenced by early Motown. Everyone has to start somewhere — and the Who never played with quite the same urgency as this, and The Jam are as contemporary as the Callaghan Government.

The music is well played and conceived — and highly commercial, with a bass riff, supplied by Bruce Foxton, holding the song together and lodging it firmly into your consciousness after one hearing. A huge hit and a record those narrow minded reactionaries who control our radio will have to play.

Walt Davidson

Corinne Cats

Weller, in his songs, responded accordingly, but admits that he didn't really know enough to offer anything worthwhile. 'I sort of meddled in politics,' he says. 'Like I just really followed The Clash and I didn't really know what the fuck I was on about.

'Really, I shouldn't have bothered with it because I didn't know what I was talking about. Some of the songs on 'In The City' were a bit political and it was really just because I was influenced by The Clash. Whereas they knew what they were talking about, I didn't have a clue.

'But all those things, regardless of what people say, were never done in a fashionable way. I did it because I believed in it, rightly or wrongly; probably most of the time, wrongly.'

At this point in their career, as far as London went, it was only fanzines such as *Bondage*, written by Shane of The Nips, who stood behind The Jam. 'I think The Jam are fucking important,' he furiously wrote. 'A lot of people don't like the suits and say they're derivative, unoriginal etc. Bollocks! There's no way you can knock their youth, their energy, their skill and their songs which are fucking great,' he concludes in classic fanzine style.

Though the majority of The Jam's repertoire was undoubtedly skilful, Weller's foray into political writing was not really a success. Songs such as 'Bricks And Mortar' are embarrassingly simplistic, stemming from Weller's uncertainty towards any fixed political stance.

'I was full of shit,' he candidly admits now.

But if he was, the success of The Jam's debut single belies such an assessment. Released on April 29th, 1977 it reached 40 in the charts after The Jam's first appearance on *Top Of The Pops*, a more than respectable position for a new group.

The success of 'City' gave them new power with their record company.

'First we did the demos,' John Weller recalls, 'then we got a deal, a pathetic deal. We had a cup of tea to celebrate. 90 days later, when 'In The City' took off, we done a bigger deal. I had looked at the contract and thought, oh fuck this, and sussed myself a lawyer who seemed to deal with a lot of music.

'That's how we did the second deal. He said that the deal was no good and I said, I know. That's why you're here. So we set up something else. He asked me what I wanted and I told him. He said, I doubt if we'll get that, but we did. A worldwide deal. From then on we never really looked back. Obviously there were ups and downs but nobody makes a million in this racket.'

To capitalise on their investment, Polydor booked The Jam into their own studios at Stratford Place with Chris Parry and Vic Smith handling production and engineering duties.

The LP took just 11 days to complete. As Rick Buckler remembers, the whole process was relatively painless. 'We had all the material,' he says, 'so when we were asked to do it we thought, great. We did it in about 11 days because it was just stuff that we had all rehearsed and we knocked it straight down. We had done some studio work before which we'd paid for ourselves, just small studios round Surrey. I mean, obviously because it was our first album we were fairly inexperienced, but I think it's good because it does capture quite truly what we were like in those days.'

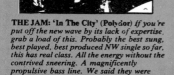

THE JAM: 'In The City' (Polydor) *If you're put off the new wave by its lack of expertise, grab a load of this. Probably the best sung, best played, best produced NW single so far, this has real class. All the energy without the contrived sneering. A magnificently propulsive bass line. We said they were gonna big big and we were right. Yah!*

THE JAM's debut album "In The City" will be released by Polydor on May 13. Of the 12 tracks, ten are original compositions by guitarist Paul Weller, and the title track is issued as a single tomorrow (Friday).

The band are currently rehearsing new material and a stage act, and next week they film a sequence for inclusion in a movie about the New Wave for British distribution in the summer.

Because of The Jam's inexperience in the recording studio, Parry basically directed the sound and feel of the LP with the group happy to take their cues from him.

'It was exciting,' says Bruce Foxton, 'because we were all so green about it. We were just in awe of it all. Let's just go in and do it, take his word as gospel until you start to learn, pick up bits and pieces. But in the early days it was a bit bewildering.'

To gain certain vocal effects on the LP, Parry even recorded some of Weller's and Foxton's vocals in the lift down the corridor, not that this helped Paul get over his initial disappointment with the LP on its completion.

'I remember taking it home the day it was finished and playing it and I was really dissatisfied with a lot of it. It didn't sound particularly authentic either way. I think it was because I was caught between this mod thing and the punk thing. The blend after a while became one thing and became the so called Jam sound I suppose, but at the time I think it fell between two stools really.'

The British public saw it in a different way. Released on May 6th, 1977, it climbed to 20 in the charts.

As far as debut albums go, 'In The City' was a faithful document of The Jam's strength and weaknesses. Because of its punk affiliations, built around a solid mod sensibility, the LP bludgeons rather than seduces with an enormous emphasis put upon the virtues of energetic playing by all the members.

The songs that succeed the best here are the ones that steer clear of political issues. 'In The City', 'Sounds From The Street', 'Away From The Numbers', 'Non-Stop Dancing' and 'I Got By In Time' all basically concern themselves with Weller's infatuation with youth, whether it be the punk scene on 'In The City', the need for individualism on 'Numbers' or the Northern Soul all-nighters on 'Non-Stop Dancing'.

It's here that Weller is able to express himself best both musically and lyrically, concocting an appealing mixture of tunes that rise above his blatant Townshend/Wilko Johnson influences and establish some kind of true identity.

At other points, the album is let down by mediocre songs such as 'Time For Truth', 'Takin' My Love', 'Bricks And Mortar' and punked-up versions of Larry Williams' 'Slow Down' and, of all things, the 'Batman Theme'.

Because of their youth and inexperience, the album tends to be one-dimensional stemming from the band's eagerness to prove themselves on vinyl. Rather than being a classic, 'In The City' lays down the seeds for the true music the band were to one day prove themselves so capable of.

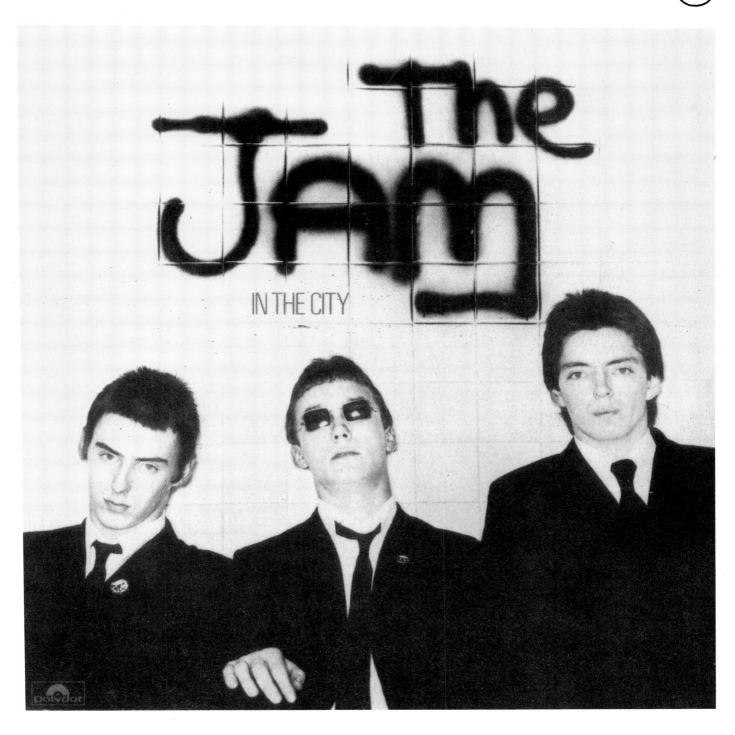

REVIEW OUTAKES ◆

'The Jam's commercial potential is enormous. Their music and image and even their infectious teen-orientated 'rebel' lyrical pose are sufficiently attractive for them to popularise New Wave to the extent where it becomes meaningless...Weller's chording is inspired, he skitters in early Townshend feedback licks with ease, he layers his guitar in a way that should be an object lesson to Wilko Johnson — he's just amazing...his songs capture that entire teen frustration vibe with the melodic grace and dynamic aplomb of early Kinks and Who...Weller's got a pretty good voice, a little like a Cockney Arthur Lee...the casual poetic edge works better than sloganeering...The acceptable face of punk rock indeed. Face it.'

Phil McNeill, NME

'The Jam are more widely accessible than just about anybody sheltering under the New Wave umbrella...and for boys who insist that nothing stronger than Vic goes up their noses, Messrs Paul Weller, Rick Buckler and Bruce Foxton certainly operate close to the speed of light...yet this album creates grave misgivings...it's a fine album but despite the high energy, Weller's raucous untreated voice, 'In The City' shows The Jam at times so close to the beat groups they're apeing that they end up like Flamin' Groovies...Paul Weller's songs are invariably built around great hooks but are too often padded out with pretty dubious non-melodies...as it is The Jam certainly have it in them to do great things but somebody's trying to get too much out of it much too soon.'

Chas de Walley, Sounds

'The Jam bear no relation to the mass conception of punk...part of today's extensive musical reaction against the dinosaur bands who have dominated rock...obvious that they have a great deal in common with The Who...considerably more than copyists...have produced tightly composed and performed songs...the Weller composed songs are anything but an embarrassment, he has a deft touch that places his material on a much higher plateau...aggressive choked off vocal and even a reference to James Brown which in itself underlines the commitment to the spirit of the early Sixties...lay down your prejudices and give them a try — they're guaranteed not to disappoint.'

Brian Harrigan, Melody Maker

'Armed and extremely dangerous The Jam stalk the decrepit grooves...if you don't like them, hard luck they're gonna be around for a long time...his sounds from the street do sound so sweet...it's been a long time since albums actually reflected pre-20 delusions and this one does.'

Barry Cain, Record Mirror

Their first British tour; four of them stuck in a red Cortina, travelling around England, from town to town, city to city. 42 dates were booked for The Jam and they managed 38 before they cancelled the rest due to exhaustion.

'We were just too fucked up,' Bruce Foxton says. 'It wasn't exactly big time. Alright we had a record out and we had done well, it was in the charts. But the places were still similar to what we'd been playing in London.'

To Weller these early dates were a drag. Not only did he find the routine of touring physically exhausting but, because of the build up in the press about the group, they would have to prove themselves each and every night to justify all the fuss.

'I haven't got any happy memories at all of the first tour,' Weller says. 'I thought they were a lot of hard and fucking painful work really. Just seemed to be touring for fucking months — it probably wasn't, just seemed that way. We were all fucked, and I was particularly fucked up.

'Mentally I was fucked up. I had just had enough of it. I enjoyed all the early club things but I never really enjoyed the way we played. I don't think we played as well on them early tours as we had in the clubs, 'cos in the clubs it's a real relaxed thing.

'We had nothing to prove. We didn't really give a shit. Onstage we'd even say it sometimes: if you don't like it you can fuck off. We really did, just do anything it was great. You're playing in a tiny room or something and we'd have one of our mates come up from Woking who'd heckle us and get this thing going, just great little spontaneous things which I found you just couldn't do on tour, I suppose because you had to go out and back up what everyone had been saying about you.'

By the end of the tour The Jam had caused enough response to play and sell out Hammersmith Odeon. Given that one of punk's main claims was to avoid bigger venues in preference to clubs, The Jam's decision to play there flew in the face of everything.

Not that they hadn't already played venues that size. A tour they had undertaken with The Clash saw The Jam pulling out of it, after playing The Rainbow, amidst a lot of inter-group bickering. It all came down to arguments concerning finance and the use of a PA. The Clash's manager Bernie Rhodes stated at the time that as they were the only two groups on the tour signed to a record company they had a duty to help out the rest of the bill which included The Buzzcocks, Subway Sect and The Slits. Rhodes said that The Jam had not given a penny and that their claim they had to pay to get on the tour was ridiculous.

'Chris Parry has claimed we demanded a four figure sum from The Jam,' said Rhodes, 'but we haven't got a penny out of them and we've lost 17,000 quid on this tour subsidising the smaller groups. But all Chris Parry and The Jam care about is themselves...'

The Jam retorted by saying that The Clash had denied them the use of a PA before The Rainbow gig, and there were suspicions that they had in fact tampered with the sound while The Jam were onstage. As for the financial details, John Weller was quoted as saying at the time, 'being asked to put our hands in our pockets all the time was how it became'.

Whatever the reasons, The Jam's headlining debut at the Hammersmith Odeon (apart from Weller falling into the pit through over eagerness) was an undoubted success, even if Paul had misgivings at the time. He could see the punk view that to play such large venues was demeaning to both band and audience, but at the same time felt that punk had to break out of the clubs for it to have maximum effect.

'I felt,' he says, 'we were getting away from a real strict idealist thing, but at the same time we couldn't have stayed in the clubs. If you kept it in the clubs it would just be like a cultist thing. What's the point in playing a club in London when it should have gone out to everyone?

'We had to spread out, and obviously by spreading out it would dissipate as well, because it couldn't remain that concentrated.'

Weller also found himself in disagreement with his father as he tried to balance his new-found idealism (now a year old) against his natural instinct to see major success for The Jam.

'In the first year,' says Paul, 'there were a lot of things that we used to row about. Well, I suppose I did really. I think my old man, at the time, felt quite insecure. I think he had this thing that he wasn't like an experienced archetypal manager. I think he thought he'd let us down possibly or not be pushing us enough.

'I think he had a little bit of an insecurity thing which only really existed in his mind because I never thought about that at all. We started to meet these people and you realise they're like the people you see in TV plays. They're actually fucking like it in real life, and I realised what a load of fucking shit it was. You take a week of it to suss out the bullshit, and I think I was really lucky that I discovered that.'

John Weller himself doubted his own ability as a manager, perhaps because of his inexperience and maybe because he didn't fully understand Paul's principles, which were — and always have been — incredibly strong.

'Sometimes I think it might have worked out better had they had a manager who came along later, like a Malcolm McLaren, a shrewdie,' John admits. 'He might have lifted them up and said, let's do this etc. I don't think I've ever come up with wonderful ideas, I've come up with safe ones, planned the tours in this country bit by bit. I've sat down and thought about it quite a lot. The first Odeon gig, nobody wanted to do that but it worked. That was the first big one, so to speak, that we did.

'Had we not have done that we would have still been fucking about in the Red Cows of this world. Simple as that.'

To complicate matters further, on their first tour Paul Weller had met a girl called Gill in Aylesbury, and for the first time in his life he'd fallen in love. They were soon seeing each other on a regular basis, but not before The Jam released their second single, 'All Around The World' c/w 'Carnaby Street'.

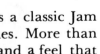

Released on July 8th, 1977 'World' still stands as a classic Jam single — a crisp, dynamic song that held no punches. More than anything on their debut LP, 'World' has a sound and a feel that caught the band perfectly with Weller's melodic, abrasive guitar providing the focal point.

Lyrically it encapsulated Weller's political train of thought in one line: '*What's the point in saying destroy? we want a new life for everyone*'. This was the message he was giving everyone.

'You've got to be realistic,' he told Brian Harrigan in *Melody Maker*. 'Just singing about anarchy isn't going to achieve anything. Even if you do change the world and overthrow everything, then what are you going to do? You still have to have leaders and so it starts all over again. There are only certain things that can be changed. Take The Sex Pistols. They've really shaken up the music industry and all the time they've just probably been laughing at everybody — especially at the media. They've made changes to the music industry but that's about it.'

Walt Davidson

Consciously or not, Weller was beginning to feel the limitations that rock, or any other art form, has when it comes to changing people's lives. The failure of punk in his view, however, wasn't going to detach him from the ideals he had set himself. Stating that the new wave was dead to Tony Parsons of *NME,* he went on to add, 'What does exist is the worth of the individual bands. *That* means something as long as they're true to themselves.'

In fact, Weller had made various attempts in that direction as the band's finances started to grow. He actually tried to give his share away.

'Well, at the time I used to get really embarrassed about getting money,' he says. 'People probably sneer at me about it, but I really did at the time. I felt it was going against the punk ideal. Around that time, I suppose it was publishing for the first LP or something, I got quite a few grand, I don't honestly know what the figure was, a lot of money as far as I was concerned being 18 or 19.

'We had a meeting with our accountants and lawyers and I said I really wanted to give my cheque away, I didn't even want it in my possession. The publisher would write it out and I'd just hand it over, give it to a fucking charity or something. They said, well even if you do that you've still got to pay tax, so I thought I'd fucking keep it then. But I would have done it at the time, I really would because it just seemed to go against everything.

'We were all on wages and I thought, well, that's it, once you've got enough to live on that's okay. I always felt guilty about having money for the first couple of years, but now I don't think about it really. I don't sit there and think I'm fucking rich, I think it's a bit pointless that. I've always been brought up that whatever you've got in your pocket is what you've got at the time.'

Not that the band were in anyway skint. 'All Around The World' reached 13 in the charts and confirmed the band's growing British audience. Abroad it was a different matter. In Europe they garnered little reaction. As for America, at the time it seemed a pointless move to tour there; but tour there they did.

Subsequently it was not the happiest of times. 'It was a drag over there,' recalls Weller. 'We played in these really crappy little clubs, doing two sets a night. I was fucked, I really was because every number in those days was just one-two-three-four for a minute and a half or something, just used to go on for like 45 minutes.

'I think it was really pretentious some of the things we had to come out with as well. We did this American press conference and I was really fucking pretentious, sort of pandering to them in a way but in a very arrogant way. Like they would say, when did this punk explosion start? and I'd say, nine o' clock tonight, or some crap like that. Of course the Yanks love all that and they'd go woah, yeah. I think in a lot of ways, in the early days I took the easy way out of a lot of things.'

The Jam played 16 American dates in 12 days and it quickly burnt the group out. It was too much too soon. 'The people from Polydor,' recalls Rick Buckler, 'turned up in New York and we were like flaked out. They thought we were being rude but we were knackered, really shagged out.

'I think we probably expected those club gigs to be very similar to the English type gigs, clubwise, and it just turned out to be something of a farce because the people in there were like a throwback from an era past. It really wasn't that good.

'The worst places were like CBGB's and the Whiskey because they were the name places. They were like trendy little clubs and it was like America's ethnic answer to punk. It was all set up, everybody in there was probably making more money than the bands were. It was that sort of game.'

What also hurt was Paul's fervent dislike of America. The gaudy commercialism, the polite falseness, the American dream and their way of life all found little comfort with this arrogant teenager who loved his homeland. On top of that he missed Gill.

'He was only 19,' says John, 'and he was missing her like fuck. Everything was getting on top of him. There were like four to five hundred kids queueing up outside the door, and shitty old places, with a curtain for a changing room and a box for a stage, to play in. And he was put off largely by having to trip around America.'

On his return from this disastrous jaunt Paul's neighbour friend, Steve Carver, popped round to see him. Asking him how he found America and his reaction to it, Weller simply replied, it sucks.

What concerned him more was his relationship with Gill.

Something of a loner anyway, Paul had started to isolate himself from friends and family as he started to experience his first true relationship with a girl. There had been girls in his life before but he found it difficult to communicate with them properly, and the affairs were usually short lived. But he was completely besotted with Gill.

'It's like whenever you meet a girl and fall in love with her or get infatuated,' Paul explains, 'it's on your mind all the time. You just eat it and sleep it.'

He was a very different Paul Weller to the cocky, troublesome character his friends were used to at the Wheatsheaf pub in Woking. Whereas before Paul would gleefully join in throwing beer at one another, upsetting tables, ripping up his clothes in public, he now sat quietly in a corner with Gill, his arm protectively around her shoulders as they huddled together.

'He'd come in and we'd all be all over in one corner mucking around,' says Steve Baker, 'and he'd come over, say hello then go and sit in the corner with Gill and just talk to her all night.'

That Paul, with his natural in-built shyness, was also becoming a public figure didn't help either.

'His family have got a tradition of having a stall at the Brookwood fete,' Steve Carver explains. 'His mum and nan do it. I remember one year he said that he wasn't going because people would come up and talk to him. His mum gave him this lecture telling him that he was hardly a household name yet. Maybe he just started getting wary of people very early. I mean, he doesn't make friends easily but once he's got a friend he sticks with them.

1. THE MODERN WORLD.
2. IN THE STREET, TODAY.
3. WIFE FROM A WINDOW. P
4. INSTANT. F
5. BRUCES.
6. HERE COMES THE WEEKEND F
7. TONIGHT AT NOON. F

1. LONDON GIRL.
2. I'M GONNA CRY. F F
3. STANDARDS.
4. LONDON TRAFFIC.
5. R+B. F
6. -
7. THE COMBINE.

'I remember going down the Wheatsheaf, after they had started doing *Top of The Pops,*' Steve continues, 'and this girl came up. It was her birthday and she had all these cards and said would you sign them all. I don't think he was very struck by it, thought she was taking the piss probably.

'Also I remember once he and Gill told me that they were walking down Oxford Street they saw these two kids. One of them had a T-shirt on which said, I Know Paul Weller and the other one had So Do I on his. Although Gill was egging him on with the story, I think he was quite pleased with it.'

Not that Paul and Gill's relationship was quite the smooth affair envisaged by romantic notions of being young and in love. Their time together, even to this day, has been plagued by constant rows and arguments as much as it has been boosted by love. Once during a blazing row at his home in Woking, rather than hit Gill, Weller smashed a tea cup over his head in frustration. His parents found him and Gill sneaking off to the hospital to have his wound attended.

'We've always had a really strange relationship,' admits Weller. 'Most people who know us think we're fucking mad. I mean, people talk about stormy relationships. . . we've always had loads and loads of rows. Funny relationship.'

It was not long before Paul and Gill moved into a flat in London's Baker Street, and Weller cut himself off completely from everything and everyone. Tired from touring with the group, infatuated with Gill, struggling to come to terms with success and the recognition it brought, his isolation brought about a change in his character.

On their return from their travels, Polydor were expecting another LP to be written and produced. First Paul had to move out of Woking, a move his parents were totally behind.

'My kids can do what they want,' says his mother, 'I only advise them. At that age you can't stop them anyway, plus the fact that if it didn't work out he could always come home. But Paul leaving home did him a lot of good because he can cook now, iron, wash, sew and it's made him much more independent which is a good thing really.'

Once ensconced in London, Weller became something of a hermit. Bruce and Rick still lived with their parents but Paul, who always hated the limitations that a small town like Woking imposed, couldn't wait to leave. The only time people would see him would be in connection with his group. Otherwise he just stayed at home with Gill watching the television. By his own admission, he was losing interest in The Jam.

'Basically, I let go of the reins,' Weller admits. 'I think meeting Gill and that fucked me up quite a lot. It really tore me between carrying on or not.'

Weller's songwriting suffered accordingly.

On their debut American tour he had begun writing material for their second LP and while still in Woking came up with a few more ideas for 'This Is The Modern World'. They weren't that good.

But it wasn't just a lapse in his creative spirit that Weller was struggling with. Ever since he began writing seriously he'd always felt the need to go one better than his contemporaries on the scene. Therefore anything other groups would come up with, Paul viewed as something of a challenge to write better material and to take some kind of creative direction from them.

By the tail-end of 1977 not a lot, in Weller's view, was happening. Bands who had first influenced him — The Clash, the Pistols — had not crystallised into what Weller had hoped they would become, and he became lost.

'There was no direction for a time,' he says. 'After that first LP and that period of time leading up to 'The Modern World', there was no real direction because the punk thing had more or less finished and I think we were all left without a direction.'

In an attempt to come up with decent songs for 'The Modern World', The Jam packed their bags and headed for a rehearsal studio in the country. 'The idea,' recalls Foxton, 'was we'd go down to this rehearsal studio, somewhere like Aylesbury, and try and bash a load of half-baked songs into shape, the idea being that because we were in the middle of nowhere we wouldn't have fuck all to do and be very productive. We just finished going up the pub every day because it just wasn't working.

'We did try but we were just forcing it. The only good news we had was when Chris Parry came in. He actually went down to the rehearsal studios at lunchtime and he asked the guy where we were, and he said probably up the pub. He came in and I think 'All Around The World' had just got in the top 20, so we had a reason to be there anyway. It was the only good bit of news to come out of that rehearsal time.'

Eventually, with Parry and Coppersmith once again producing, the band recorded their second LP. By now, with Paul wrapped up in Gill and living in London, the social bond between the three of them was gradually disappearing.

'Probably started happening when he met Gill,' claims Bruce. 'It could have been any other way round, if Rick or myself had met a girl. It was more like then when we started drifting apart. I think out of the three of us, I was probably closer to Paul, I got on better I suppose, but then once he met Gill it started to drift apart for obvious reasons.'

Bruce felt threatened by Gill's presence and her effect on Paul. Sometimes he found the affair amusing. 'Modern World' we recorded at Island. Paul was crazy about Gill and he was disappearing every five minutes with her out of the studio. You know, where the fuck is he?'

At other times he found it disconcerting. 'I think I was probably a bit concerned at the time thinking, would the songwriting suffer? But obviously there was nothing you could do. It's up to him. The friendship suffered a bit; well, a lot, like the old cliché love is blind, but there's fuck all you can do. I wouldn't want either Rick or Paul interfering in my life.

'Obviously it affected the touring, the laughs dwindled because you've got your missus on tour, all that side went a bit by the board. The main concern was, like don't neglect the songwriting, and if he had of done, what could we do about it? It was up to him to realise it.'

On October 10th, 1977, The Jam's third single 'The Modern World' c/w live versions (from the 100 Club) of 'Sweet Soul Music' and 'Back in My Arms Again' was released.

After the exhilaration of 'All Around The World', this third single came as something of a disappointment. Nicking the main riff from The Who's 'Pictures of Lily', The Jam sound angry and concerned but not convincing enough to carry the song fully. A step sideways rather than forward, it could only reach 36 in the charts before dropping.

By then the 'This Is The Modern World' LP was on release.

The Jam's first venture in surrealist
, this pose was Paul's idea.

Rick 'n' Rat

Confused, directionless and misplaced, 'This Is The Modern World' saw The Jam in their worst light. It is, quite simply, a bad album. Lacking the spirit of their debut LP even, Weller's songs here were either too busy apeing old Who riffs — 'Modern World' and 'Standards' — or splashing about in a pool of average songwriting.

Occasionally there were flashes of inspiration; 'London Girl' and 'Tonight At Noon' were potentially good pop songs if developed properly. But most of the LP, which suffers from a murky production, still remains completely unconvincing.

Bruce Foxton, who wrote 'Carnaby Street' on the B-side of 'All Around The World', contributed two songs on the album: 'London Traffic' is a cringe (how can one get so passionate about something as dull and obvious as traffic in London?) and 'Don't Tell Them You're Sane' is like a third form essay about a mental patient.

Nor does Weller contribute anything of any note lyrically, either dropping in clichés — *'The Kids want some action and who can fucking blame them?'* ('In The Street Today' co-written with Dave Waller), or *'Don't hang around and be foolish, do something constructive with your weekend!'* ('Here Comes The Weekend') — or unimaginatively stating the obvious.

Musically and lyrically, it's hardly the stuff of giants. The British public agreed. Released on November 4th, 1977, it reached 22 in the charts before slipping away.

'The Who's influence is marked on both the construction of the songs and the instrumental style...much of the record suffers precisely because it's typical Jam — 'Standards', 'Here Comes The Weekend', 'In The Street Today' and 'Modern World' are all adequate but thoroughly ordinary and don't represent any development...some of the songs are lyrically weak... 'Standards' seems to ridicule the kind of Tory attitude Weller once espoused, which is fine but the attack is too glib and exaggerated...existence does have its highs and it's when Paul Weller is glorying in it that he seems to write his best...The Jam spiriting us towards the second psychedelic age?...Paul Weller should mature into one of our best songwriters, provided he keeps his mind open...this album only hints at what The Jam are capable of.'

Chris Brazier, Melody Maker

'And people were trying to tell me that this was a lousy album and The Jam were all washed up... it's one of the best albums I've heard in a long time... admittedly Paul Weller's voice still leaves a lot to be desired... not everything here owes a debt to The Who... The Jam capture the essence of transistor radio rock. Bright and naive. Timeless. Brilliant... Weller is a dry and impassive observer... in some cases you might even call him genuinely and humanely perceptive... The Jam are streets ahead of their rivals... The Jam are young and brave... still as real and ingenious as it is possible to be in the rock business... as a live band they are quite one of the best... it still isn't their masterpiece.'

Chas de Walley, Sounds.

'So this is the modern world. I'm glad they told me. For an instant I'd thought I'd been transported back to 1965... he doesn't need me to tell him (Weller) that The Jam are playing excellent, streamlined rock and roll. He also won't want me to point out that the production by Vic Smith and Chris Parry is well on the thin side, that some of the riffs don't stand up to the amount of repetition that they are subjected to and that after a couple of tracks the vocals do lean towards the monotonous... what The Jam have in common with the rest of the British new wave is a kind of sullen gut level nihilism... I doubt anything I could say would add to or detract from its obvious status as a hot item, buywise. So roll the commercials.'

Mick Farren, NME

'Forget the sixties. Forget comparisons. Forget Jam, The Who, Beatles, The Kinks. Forget the naive neurosis of the plagiarists. The Jam are here. And now...'This Is The Modern World' reflects a definite PROGRESSION (remember that?) a definite identity mould...here Weller is making an obvious attempt at creating a Jam SOUND. He succeeds. Brilliantly. It is in fact a ceremonial uncovering of the post-pubescent metropolitan veil - moth eaten but nonetheless sacrosanct...the name of the game is simplicity...it's not that Weller is softening, it's just that he's learning...his cracked pavement voice has often been a cause for concern in certain circles which I could never understand. It's perfect for his songs...he sings like he looks. Freddie Garrity could never say that...'

Barry Cain, Record Mirror

If 'This Is The Modern World' represented The Jam at their lowest creative level, then there didn't seem a lot that either Weller, Foxton or Buckler could do to alter that situation.

As a songwriter Paul had dried up completely, Foxton's material was hardly spectacular and Buckler, after a few cursory attempts, had realised that he couldn't write songs at all. Quite simply, the situation was getting increasingly fragile and the band were now growing further apart as friends.

'I think we became a little separated by the time I had met Gill,' says Paul. 'I just totally immersed myself with her, so therefore we weren't as close. I wanted to take her on tour with me, the whole thing. All a real mistake when you look back at it, to cut yourself off that completely, but there you go, things happen that way. We weren't as close as what we had been before and that's my fault really.'

To promote 'Modern World' The Jam undertook another British tour. One night in Leeds, Paul and Bruce ran into some rugby players staying at the same hotel. They ended up brawling with them.

'We were standing up to get some drinks,' recalls Bruce, 'and some words were exchanged. The next minute Paul was in a bit of a ruck and I tried to help him out. He just finished up being like a rugby ball. They went berserk. They went mad. It really was frightening. They were after our blood, literally, and we had to leave about three in the morning check into another hotel. It fucked the rest of the tour because I had badly bruised ribs.'

The fracas ensured that Paul Weller had to make an appearance at Leeds Crown Court where he was greeted on the steps by a message some fans had scrawled: 'Paul Weller Is Innocent'. 'He was and was discharged straight away.

Concluding the tour at Christmas with another show at the Hammersmith Odeon, Weller again retreated to his London flat, disillusioned.

Whereas before the press had been on his side, with the release of 'Modern World' they turned against him, and it threw Weller. Relatively small sales of the LP compounded his feelings. But for Rick Buckler, The Jam's second LP was something that they had to do, to show everyone that they had more inside them than just straight forward punk anthems.

'I think people expected something more on the lines of 'In The City', and when 'Modern World' came out it was a bit of a culture shock. We didn't want to say, oh, the first album has done well, all we'll do is just reproduce it, we wanted to explore our own capabilities a lot more.

'But even though people say 'Modern World' wasn't a great success, I think it was an album that we couldn't have done without really. If we hadn't done it then the lessons that we learnt would be gone. I don't know what would have happened because it really made us think. So even though it was a bit of a shakey album, it was good for us to do. I don't think I would have liked to have seen it done any other way because we learned a lot from that.'

Two months into 1978, The Jam put out their fourth single, 'News of the World' c/w 'Aunties And Uncles' and 'Innocent Man'. Only 'Aunties' was a Weller original, the other two songs written by Bruce, emphasising Weller's sterile phase.

Once again it was an average single from the group, Bruce's forced lyrics letting down the song as a whole. 'Aunties' was pithy rubbish, a song Weller had written at least a year before, and 'Innocent Man' was the kind of material that third rate new wave groups were coming up with. Released on February 24th, it gained a respectable position in the charts, 27, but didn't bode well for the future.

By then, though, The Jam were back in the States, supporting Blue Oyster Cult and going down like lead balloons in front of audiences brought up on a staple diet of Led Zeppelin and the like. It all seemed pointless: trudging around the States for five weeks with every show greeted by derision.

America always depressed Paul, although Bruce and Rick took to it more, despite the hostile reception they were receiving. 'A lot of things,' Paul says, 'seemed to be going wrong like that at the time. We were just getting into really stupid situations like that, supporting Blue Oyster Cult; totally fucking pointless.'

On their return home the group began putting new material for their third album together. On their ill-fated jaunt around America Paul had written a few new songs, and Bruce had come up with some titles too. In England they rehearsed and demo'd the songs, but Weller still seeemed nonchalant about the group.

'It wasn't so much being lazy,' he says, 'but I just lost interest. As I said, I let go of the reins and I wasn't particularly interested in picking them up any more. So we were just running through these songs, doing these demos, and I was just going along with it really.'

It was to be Chris Parry who finally shook Weller out of his complacency. He came down to the studio, heard the new songs and told the group what he thought.

'His actual words were, this is shit,' recalls Weller. 'And in that instance he was right. It was good that someone actually came out and said it. I think Bruce was a little choked because a lot of the songs were his, but my songs were terrible as well. Once somebody actually came out and said it, though, it was like a big relief really.'

Scrapping the stuff that they had recorded, Paul then moved back to Woking to live with his parents for a while because he and Gill had been forced to move out of their London flat.

It was the first time he'd been home in ages. 'I never went back to Woking for months and months, till about maybe a year,' he states. 'And I never went out with other people. I never mixed, I never spoke to other people at all, even within the band, and I think that makes you really lose the open-mindedness that maybe you had before.'

The move back to his home town, albeit for a short while, coupled with the precarious position of The Jam, pushed Weller back into concentrating on his talents more fully. At the time, the general feeling was that creatively The Jam were finished, their days numbered. The situation was exacerbated further by a statement Bruce Foxton made to a *Sounds* reporter on the group's mini-tour prior to recording their third album.

'I don't know whether it's going to work out,' he is reported as saying during what he thought was a private conversation in a late night disco, and which was not intended for the record. 'But one thing I do know is that when The Jam fall through I ain't gonna join another band. This is the only band I'll ever play with.

'I wouldn't want to go through all that hustling round the clubs again, and I wouldn't want it to be a case of Bruce 'who used to be in The Jam' Foxton's new band. No, what I want is to get a small business of my own. I'd really like to open up a guesthouse or a small hotel. I've seen all these people open up one year with just four or five rooms, the next year it's seven or eight, then the next year they're having an extension built. You can't go wrong. I've got a bit of money saved up and when it all falls through — which could be tomorrow, who knows? — that's what I think I'll do. Open up a place.'

To be rambling on like a failed musician making his last will and testament showed how far Foxton's confidence had sunk. 'I was a bit concerned,' he says, 'because you are sort of wondering. Paul had all the songs and I was worried as to whether he could come up with it again. I really enjoyed what he was doing, but you had to come up with the goods because otherwise we were going to be out on our ears. At that time it was because we thought that's it then, he hasn't got anything to offer. But he has periods anyway when he just dries up, which obviously we know about.'

◆

If his own group were starting to doubt his ability, along with the rest, then it was clearly a make or break time for Weller. Not only was there pressure from outside sources — namely Polydor — but everything that the group had worked towards would now seem a complete waste of time.

Weller, with his back against the wall, responded by producing a batch of songs that were quite easily the best of his career till then. Somehow his stay in Woking, coupled with the weight upon his shoulders, had brought him out of his shell both musically and personally.

Where previously he had become arrogant to hide his growing disinterest, he now emerged with a clear perspective, determined to prove that he wasn't washed up.

The Jam's first move, in that direction, was to drop Chris Parry as producer. 'For a variety of different reasons,' explains Weller. 'I mean, the sound we weren't happy with it. Both him and Vic fucked up with 'The Modern World', it could have been a lot better production, it would have been better. We thought they really fucked it up.

'Chris didn't really do an awful lot. He had some good ideas but technically he didn't really know, which is okay sometimes, but not when people are taking money out of you. There were other things that Chris helped with, like when he came in and said that the songs we were doing were shit. It was good that someone was there. Vic was the sort of person who would just let it carry on and hope the group would find itself, so I think Chris was helpful in that way, but that was basically it.

'I think Rick and Bruce were really pissed off that he had slagged those songs. It hit them a little bit more than me really. I agreed with him.'

In fact, Parry's presence on the early sessions, according to Bruce, was something of a hindrance. 'It was like a stalemate halfway through,' Foxton explains. 'It's only if you've got a producer, one producer and you can bounce ideas off each other, but with that there were three different things going on. It was just getting a bit too confusing. Chris was suggesting this, we were suggesting doing something else. Someone had to go. We were getting too much at loggerheads all the time and instead of it being positive it was negative.

'The thing was, Chris had his ordinary job as well and we'd be in the studio working all day and then he'd probably come in late in the evening and say, no, I don't like that, and it was really slowing us down. It was just unnecessary because we were having more say in what we wanted, so it had to be accepted in the end.'

Accepted it was, and with just Vic-Coppersmith-Heaven producing, The Jam embarked on recording their all-important third album.

'We got a couple of songs going and we really did realise that it was happening again. It was a good feeling recording 'All Mod Cons', I suppose because it was a vital, really important time, shit or bust sort of album,' Bruce Foxton recalls. 'We really wanted to prove that we didn't want to be written off with 'Modern World', so it was one of the most challenging, exciting sessions we've done.'

Two singles preceded the release of 'All Mod Cons'. August 8th 1978, saw the release of 'David Watts' c/w 'A Bomb in Wardour Street'; the A-side was a sparkling cover version of a Kinks song (by dint of them playing it live so much it actually became a Jam song in a sense), and the flipside a terse number with a recurring, appealing riff that showed Weller re-capturing some of his old talent. It reached 25 in the charts and was immediately followed by 'Down In The Tube Station At Midnight' c/w 'So Sad About Us' (an old Who song The Jam used to play and recorded as a tribute to Keith Moon who had just died), and 'The Night', a Bruce Foxton composition.

If 'A-Bomb' had shown Weller back on the track, 'Tube Station' confirmed beyond all doubt his ability. It's a stunning song.

Relating the story of a man viciously attacked on a tube, Weller covers all points on this song — from the dramatic edge he brings to his vocal performance, the jagged chords that ring out from his guitar and the touches of perception he brings to the lyrics, adding colour and drama.

It was on this song that he really came into his own, and its basic ingredients he was to use for the next year and a half, creating characters and painting vivid, detailed portraits of them over some great pop music.

'A lot of my songs,' he explains, 'start off as visual ideas (I would say 80% of them do) and I see the songs in terms of little films in my head. This is probably why a lot of them have conclusions. They're not all essentially about me. Some I use characters in situations, and 'Tube Station' is one of those.

'The original idea was to try and write a short TV play, only in a three minute music context. The song came from my own neurosis, as a lot do, and the lyrics I wrote really quickly. At first they were written as a short story. I later split them up into lines and chopped bits out here and there. It's always amused me how the songs most people think of as my best were written so quickly.'

'Down In The Tube Station At Midnight' was released on October 6th 1978, and reached an encouraging 15 in the charts. The week after it came out, 'All Mod Cons' was released.

The Jam's renaissance had begun.

Bristling with talent and imagination, 'All Mod Cons' stands as one of the premier LPs of the late '70s. Eleven out of 12 songs Weller originals, 'Mod Cons' is a tight, cohesive LP and one which saw Paul Weller finally imbue The Jam with their own distinctive sound and style.

Whereas before he was content to allow his Who infatuation to take over, here he hones down his influences and creates his own startling identity. The music is uplifting and forceful, the words colourful and dramatic. Both contain an edge which complement each other perfectly, creating real moods of tension and anger, peace and tranquility.

Embellished throughout with subtlety, 'Mod Cons' thrives on a vitality that Weller seemed to have misplaced on previous outings. There's the bitter attacking guitar on 'Billy Hunt', the chilling menace of 'Mr Clean', the bitter twist of 'To Be Someone' and the slightly embarrassing 'English Rose', written for and about, Gill, and not even mentioned on the lyric sheet or album cover.

Most of the LP's themes concern themselves with ideals and dreams, never realised, often broken, hence Weller's penchant for inventing characters, — Billy Hunt, Mr Clean, the victims portrayed in 'Tube Station' and 'Someone', and writing around them with an understanding and perception that few possess.

By doing this, and allying them to some inspired music, he touched a responsive nerve in most young people from all backgrounds. He also, by dint of his style, found himself accused of sitting on the fence by not stating his viewpoint, but on 'All Mod Cons' just the tone of his voice is enough to show where his sympathies lie.

He, along with Bruce and Rick supplying an emphatic backing, forged from all their years together, manages here to provide a collection of songs that are still relevant and playable today, that provide a humane insight into most people's lives without ever being condescending and still shine with an appealing energy and spirit. Things could only get better from here.

REVIEW OUTAKES

'It's not only several light years ahead of anything they've ever done before but also the album that is going to catapult The Jam right into the front rank of international rock and roll; one of the handful of truly essential rock albums of the last few years...Weller has transcended his original naivety without becoming cynical about anything other than the music business...'All Mod Cons' is an album based firmly in 1978 and looking forward...Weller has the almost unique ability to write love songs that convince the listener that the singer is *really in love*...Weller is — like Bruce Springsteen — tough enough to break down his own defences, secure enough to make himself vulnerable...this is as good a place as any to point out that bassist Bruce Foxton and drummer Rick Buckler are more than equal to the new demands that Weller is making on them: the vitality, empathy and resourcefulness they display throughout the album makes 'All Mod Cons' a collective triumph for The Jam as well as a personal triumph for Weller...if these songs mean that one less meaningless street fight gets started then we'll all owe Paul Weller a favour...it'll be the album that makes The Jam *real* contenders for the crown. Look out all you rock and rollers; as of now The Jam are the ones you have to beat.'

Charles Shaar Murray, NME.

'Must have been the pressure and frustration that drove Weller into creating 'All Mod Cons'...they just blast away 12 years of blind-alley 'progression' and take up the mantle of Townshend/Lennon-McCartney for the modern world...Weller translates his thematic concerns into his finest lyrics to date...to describe the album in more than 400 words is a nonsense.'

Garry Bushell, Sounds.

'Forget the crash, bang, wallop revivalist style of their early days; The Jam have come of age...they are not imitators but upholders of a great British tradition...this is Sixties music handled in an original and modern way which has given The Jam their distinctive and now truly distinguished style...no clever final comments, just that this is one of three albums of '78.'

Philip Hall, Record Mirror.

'Starving the market of vinyl product is not a game which you can accuse The Jam of playing...perhaps if Paul Weller were to be a little less enthusiastic, a little less concerned with churning out singles like a bottle factory, The Jam would not be in danger of becoming tiresome...not that Weller can't still pull a gem or two...Weller has got himself into an essentially sterile trap...if it wasn't for the fact that Weller is so obviously sincere it would be an insult ('English Rose')...basically nothing has changed musically except Weller has moved on a year or two. By this rate, taking into account the hyper-active output, he should have caught up with the rest of us in 1990. Can you wait?'

Frances Lass, Melody Maker.

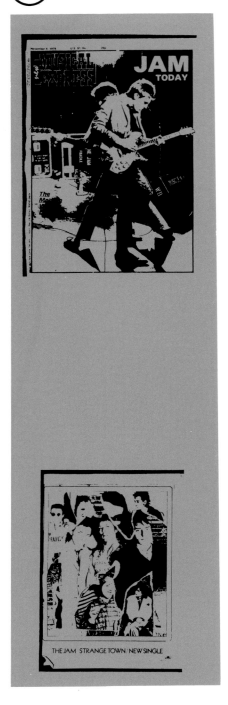

Success affects in different ways. Looking back over pop's history, the books are littered with the casualties, the obscenities, the accidents, all caused by the thrust into the spotlight.

Weller was more than aware of the pitfalls. On 'To Be Someone' he had summed up his thoughts on the matter and promised both himself and others that he would never get above the people he was playing to.

It's no surprise then that The Jam became something of an insular thing. Paul writing songs, his father managing them, sister Nicky running the fan club before Ann Weller took it over. It's almost as if Paul needed his world, which also included Gill, before he could face his own responsibilities.

There's a definite need in Paul for a secure base to work from and the ideals he had picked up on from the punk era — the refusal to play out the rock star, to be as accessible as possible — are as much a part of that as anything. His modernist stance also provided him with an identity.

With 'All Mod Cons', The Jam moved into the major league; it reached six in the charts and with it came the *real* pressure.

'I've always got mixed feelings about success,' says Weller. 'It's like Malcom Muggeridge saying that some days you go out and you get recognised a lot and it can really do you in. Then other days you'll go out and nobody will recognise you and you'll get annoyed. You think, fuck, what's happening? You don't even necessarily mean it to be. At the same time, the worst aspect of it is that it really gets to your ego and sometimes you really like it even though you don't really need it, it just affects you that way.'

Certainly Weller, more than anyone else really, has gone out of his way not to be affected by the position he'd fought his way to, and with the artistic and commercial success of 'Mod Cons' behind him, he finally found a new leash of confidence.

'To me that'll be like *the* first Jam record, the one where we found our sound and made us important. I felt this group has got to be taken seriously now, not just Who derivatives. I thought it was a really important record, and I still do.'

Where previously Weller had replaced his confidence in himself with a negative, cocky arrogance, he could now drop it and expect the acclaim and respect he so patently deserved.

'I just decided from that point to try and always do things properly and never let go of the fucking reins again, which I don't think I've done since that time.'

Following successful tours both in Britain and Europe, The Jam re-surfaced with a new single 'Strange Town' c/w 'The Butterfly Collector'. Released on March 5th, 1979, the sound Vic Coppersmith-Heaven had given the band was a lot tougher than anything on 'Mod Cons'. The story of an alien who lands in Britain, the lyrics are barely decipherable, the excitement and energy of the song sweeping it along.

Weller's songs were now becoming more rounded, and the B-side, 'Butterfly Collector' — a slow, haunting, bitter piece about a club owner — was proof of his growing confidence and talent. It was the first of many classy B-sides The Jam were to produce and which wouldn't surface on LPs, an ideal that Weller has always stuck to.

In interviews, however, Weller seemed less articulate than his music would suggest. As the main songwriter,most journalists made a bee-line for him, only to find a sullen, reserved, nervous 20 year old who thought that all the answers were in his songs anyway.

For Foxton and Buckler it was a different matter. 'There was never any resentment,' says Rick about the publicity Paul was getting. 'If they had talked to me it would have been more boring because what I could have told them was probably very little, you know. As far as actual good reading makes, obviously you want to know more than what the drummer sees.'

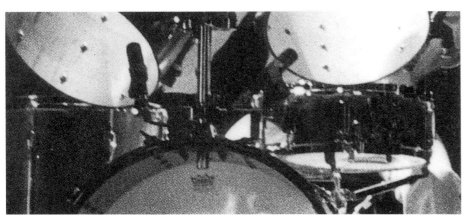

What Weller was telling journalists, especially Harry Doherty in a *Melody Maker* interview, was that at 20 he felt too old. It was said as a reaction to the shoddy groups he saw around him, bands like 999 and Sham 69, with their populist pub rants and chants.

'I've always taken things seriously, taken things literally and that's probably one of my faults,' admits Paul, 'but with Pursey saying things like kids like you and me, it just disgusted me because I really believed in the punk thing, that it was teenagers who counted.

'For someone to pretend to be teenage, and there were a lot doing that, using that punk thing when they were ancient, just used to annoy me so much. I just wanted to make some comment, clarification about the importance of teenagers.

'Punk without teenagers was a joke to me. It's just a thing I've got, something I've always had in my mind. Like that pact I made with myself that if I didn't make it by the time I was 20 I'd give up, and crossing that bit between being a teenager and not being one really frightened me. I worried that we'd lose something. Whatever I had, I'd lose it.'

Compared to the likes of Pursey, Paul Weller was undoubtedly streets ahead in words and music. Even if The Jam with their direct comments on youth and Britain were reaching a similar audience, he was in no way appealing to the rabble rousing mentality that Pursey was exploiting and finally couldn't contain. Instead, Weller's songs drew a close analogy to the '60s Pop Art movement — as he told John Hamblett in the *NME*.

'I've read a few books on Pop Art and I think it had a lot in commom with the punk thing. Before the Pop Artists came along, there were the Expressionists who were just dealing with their own very self-indulgent art, but the Pop Artists brought into art everyday images that ordinary people could relate to. Which is why it really interests me. I see The Jam along those lines, using things that everybody knows are there but presenting them in a different art form.'

With 'Mod Cons' Weller had certainly achieved that aim and with the release of their eight single, 'When You're Young' c/w a Bruce Foxton song (the best he's ever written) 'Smithers Jones', went further in defining this direction.

Once again tackling familiar themes — youth and disillusionment — Weller's pen was typically penetrating and acidic. *'You think you're a king but you're really a pawn. . .it's so hard to comprehend why they set up your dreams to have them smashed in the end. . .the world is your oyster but you're future's a clam, it's got you in your grips before it's born.'*

Where most pop singles try to celebrate youth, Weller could never pretend that all was rosy, and his cynicism (which was to take him over later in the year) often caught the mood of the people he was attracting.

Words like 'spokesman' and 'youth leader' started being bandied around, and although it was a position that Paul Weller instinctively shunned, he seemed the only young musician capable of articulating the hopes and fears of his audience. By not acting out a cliché existence as a 'rock star', his experiences and unnerving knack of pinpointing a mood or train of thought, endeared him not only to a solid block of working class youth but to people from all kinds of backgrounds.

His refusal to sing in an Americanised accent, as some of his contemporaries were doing, also kept The Jam uniquely British, but then this isn't surprising. There's not only frustration and anger in Weller's character but a large romantic streak which responds not only to love but to picturesque English scenery, something that 'The Place I Love' tried to define on 'All Mod Cons'.

His Britishness also surfaces in his love of modernism which in the summer of '79 was revived as a youth movement with the emergence of such mod groups as Secret Affair, The Merton Parkas and The Chords.

The Jam, because of Weller's much publicised mod lifestyle, were cast as the leaders of the movement, but Weller refused to be drawn.

Having seen the problems first hand of aligning yourself with any one cause or movement, as he had done in the punk days, a firm pledge to what was basically a second rate, even desperate movement, could only harm The Jam and even alienate their growing audience. Apart from that, Rick and Bruce had never been that struck by modernism in the first place. For the sake of image (Foxton, in fact, only had his reasonably long hair cropped after signing with Polydor) the pair of them adopted mod-type clothing but never with Paul's conviction.

To Weller the only thing that appealed about this mod movement was that there was a new breed of young bands around, some of whom — Purple Hearts, The Chords — he found acceptable. Not that he had a lot of time to fully check them out because he was constantly touring in England and abroad. A major British tour was followed by jaunts to Europe, the States, Canada and then back again for a mini-tour of the UK to promote the new single.

It's not surprising that they undertook such a heavy schedule. The Jam onstage were always a different proposition to The Jam on vinyl. On a good night, there were few who could touch them for sheer, committed playing. Not only did the tension and dynamics of their playing come fully into focus, but the frustration and anger, especially in Weller, became clearly visible, adding even more excitment to their music.

Weller's need for communication, his driving force, made even more sense in front of an audience receptive to his every move, whilst Foxton and Buckler were more than capable of supplying the backdrop for Weller's burning passion, a passion that translated itself perfectly from a stage.

Ever conscious of the mistakes made by groups before him, Weller always made sure that their live set never featured material older than a year, always inserting newer, unrecorded material where possible or delivering cover versions of songs by The Four Tops, Small Faces, etc.

In the studio, however, things were much different. For the first two albums the group had just basically gone in, played live and fiddled around with the recorded tapes afterwards, adding or subtracting bits, with either Chris Parry or Vic Coppersmith helping out Paul with arrangements.

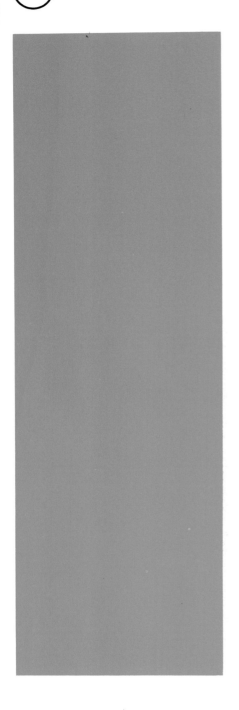

'Something like 'All Around The World',' says Paul, 'Chris Parry arranged and he totally changed the song, which was good. Vic liked some of the singles like 'Strange Town' which he sort of arranged and did a good job on. A lot of those songs at the time, I was just taking him really bare and we'd gradually build it up.'

Vic Coppersmith-Heaven spent 15 hours mixing 'Tube Station' and two days on 'Strange Town', examples of the lengths he was prepared to go to. For the group it was a different way to how they'd experienced recording before, and in many ways they felt it was diluting the sound they were after.

'A lot of our material,' Bruce Foxton remarks, 'has always come out better on a stage because it finds its level after a few weeks of playing it, you get the true feel of the song and nine times out of ten it works better. With recording, though, it's trying to find the right moment to record a number.'

On 'When You're Young' the band had already recorded two versions, which Vic and the group weren't happy with. As they prepared to move to another studio to get a proper version completed, Polydor asked Paul, John and Vic in to a meeting.

'We'd spent four to five thousand pounds,' explains Coppersmith-Heaven, 'and we weren't satisfied with either of the versions we'd done, so I was about to try a third different studio because I thought The Jam were in a good situation where they could plan and wait rather than rushing out something that wasn't right. I was pulled in for a meeting along with Paul and John and I was told I didn't know what I was doing. The managing director of Polydor told me that it was quite possible I wouldn't produce The Jam again. There was talk of an American producer.

'Naturally I was pissed off. But Paul was fantastic. I couldn't have had a better friend. He stood by me totally, and although I don't think the Polydor people understood at all, they had to go along with him.'

Although Paul might have stuck by Vic in this instance, the recording sessions the group began for their fourth album, were not to their liking. For a start, Paul didn't have enough material for a full LP, so instead of the usual process of demoing the song on tape and then rehearsing it before actually recording, the group were forced to record anything he wrote straight away, almost cold.

There was also pressure on the band to complete it as quickly as possible, so as to be able to fulfil the commitments they had for the next year. Weller, in fact, was writing a lot of the songs in the studio with Bruce and Rick learning their parts at night, before Paul came back into the studio.

'I wasn't sure what was going on,' admits Foxton. 'We were just sort of learning it and recording it at the same time, and personally I was just concentrating on what I was playing as opposed to what it really sounded like. We were literally learning it one night and recording it the next day, which is pretty fatal to do. Invariably you're going to listen to it in a few days time and think, oh, I wish I'd done that, and that would have been better.'

By recording like this the actual cost of the LP rose as the days went by, but Weller, always looking for a challenge to motivate himself, enjoyed the pressure of writing in this way. Songs such as 'Thick As Thieves' and 'The Eton Rifles' (written in his family's caravan at Selsey Bill whilst on holiday) were already finished before he entered the studio. Others he had to make up on the spot: 'Private Hell', for instance.

'That's quite funny really,' he says about it. 'Just sat down and wrote it because we needed some more songs for the LP, and it's a good song really. But a lot of things are easy to do like that because you've already got your ideas anyway. All I needed was someone to say well, you've got to have this finished by next Tuesday, and so I would do it.'

The care and attention that Vic Coppersmith wanted to pay the album also slowed them up, but eventually The Jam's ninth single 'The Eton Rifles' c/w 'See-Saw' was released on October 22nd, 1979. It was their first top five hit, eventually reaching number three in the charts, and deservedly so.

Crashing in on a chaotic rumble of feedback it quickly sorts itself out into a classic pop form, choc-a-bloc with little riffs and ideas that added up to a rousing song. To Weller, the lyrics were intended as half-humorous statements about class warfare, a subject close to his heart; but there's no mistaking the bitterness in his voice when he spits out the ironic, *what a catalyst you turned out to be*.

But then the material he had come up with for 'Setting Sons', for the main part, was brimming with irony and despair. Far from relaxing in his new found role as a major songwriter, it seemed that success had spurred him into an even more cynical frame of mind. Weller himself believes that cynicism is an inbuilt characteristic of his, and a complex one at that.

'For me to write really optimistic songs,' he states, 'I've really got to detach myself a little bit from my own personality, because however much I try not to get in that frame of mind, I get a lot of really bad bouts of depression so it just comes out in the songs. There is a little bit of that manic depressive in me. If I'm depressed I'm really down, everything just seems useless and I don't know why I'm like that, it's just a state of mind. Like I've never had any real big traumas. Never anything that say Steve Brookes went through with his parents, so if anything it should be other people.

'Maybe it's because I do see things in very simple terms. I see a lot of crap going down, which is totally unnecessary, in all areas, and it just frustrates me. The solutions are so simple, or to me they appear simple, when in fact there's fuck all you can do about it, just this overwhelming wall of establishment.'

If anything, the bitterness Weller displayed on 'Setting Sons' was more than proof of this trait in him. It was finally released on October 27th, 1979, and reached their highest position yet, four in the charts.

To The Jam it was their worst album ever. 'I was really unhappy with 'Setting Sons',' admits Weller. 'To me it was a real let down. It could have been another group. The sound was really horribly professional, on the verge of being slick. I was never particularly pleased with it.'

Weller's original idea for the LP was to have a main theme running throughout concerning the lives of three boys who grew up together. To that purpose, songs like 'Thick As Thieves' and 'Burning Sky' were penned, but because Weller didn't have the time to write the rest of the material, songs such as 'Girl On The Phone' were quickly knocked out. Also included was an orchestrated version of Foxton's 'Smithers Jones', which had first surfaced as a B-Side to 'When You're Young'.

'It was Rick's idea to put an orchestral backing to it,' says Foxton. 'I was well into the idea, I wanted to see all these musicians playing on a song of mine. I don't know if it really achieved anything, but I think I probably preferred the band's version though it was really interesting to see the guys in there anyway.'

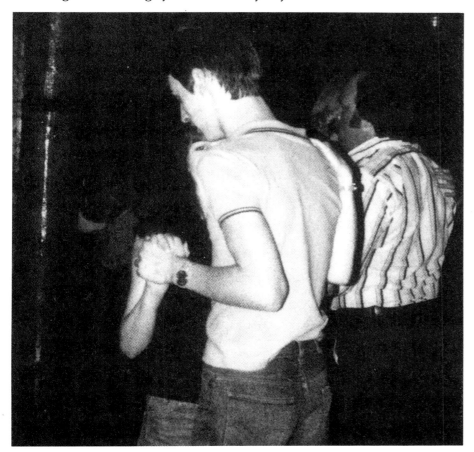

For many people, 'Setting Sons' remains their favourite Jam LP. It's not hard to understand why. Compared to the slightly muted sound of 'Mod Cons', The Jam's fourth album leaps out with a harsh invigorating, brutal sound. Weller, ever conscious of the need to progress, imbues his songs here with comparatively complicated arrangements that, for the most part, work. Also his lyrics are amongst the best he's written, taking each subject and writing about them with added depth.

The themes are familiar — observations on England past, present and future. The songs written around his idea about three boys growing apart, are easy to spot: 'Thick As Thieves', a penetrating look at male relationships, *thick as thieves as us, we'd stick together for all times, and we meant it but it turns out just for a while, we stole the friendship that bound us together*; 'Little Boy Soldiers' with its three movements, ambitious in the extreme and Weller talented enough to pull it off; 'Wasteland' with its resigned fatality as the friends sit amongst the ruins — *and when or if the sun shines, lighting our once beautiful features, we'll smile but only for seconds, for to be caught smiling is to acknowledge life, a brave, but useless show of compassion and that is forbidden in this drab and colourless world*; and 'Burning Sky', the bitter story of a man caught up in commerce, unable to communicate to his ex-friends anymore.

It's these songs, along with 'Saturday Kids' and its frightening lyrics of *mums and dads smoke Capstan non-filters, wall paper lives cause they all die of cancer*, 'Private Hell' and the brilliant 'The Eton Rifles' that show Weller unflinchingly portraying lives and emotions set within a typically British context.

It was as if Weller, so caught up in his love of Britain, its people and characteristics, had to resolve the ugly side of it before he could accept the goodness it had to offer. Foxton, on the other hand, paints an unexpected, sympathetic portrait of the archetypal British businessman in 'Smithers Jones', though Weller's last verse adds the familiar, bitter twist amongst the sweet harmonies of the strings: *It's time to relax now you've worked your arse off, but the only one smilin' is the sun tanned boss, work and work and work and work till you die, there's plenty more fish in the sea to cry.*

'Setting Sons' offers no solutions, paints unbelievably bleak scenarios fuelled by Weller's despair at the fragility of friendships, the futility of protest, the harrowing lives people are forced to live and meekly accept without thinking. Weller, his voice improving tremendously, sees both sides of the coin. *It's the system, hate the system,* he implores on 'Saturday Kids', before adding, with a resigned tone, *what's the system?*

He had now grown enough to realise that despite the inherent promise that rock music offers of liberation and freedom, there are never any easy answers or solutions and certainly none that any guitar, bass or drum could ever come up with.

He was 21 at the time.

THE JAM - No. 1 in your hearts

Marc Zaloman

'Weller is unlikely to self-destruct because he's far too clever by far...'Setting Sons' is a major development and something of a departure. Basically The Jam are disassociating themselves from mod before they're buried with it...there isn't one dubious song among the nine originals...the album is still the greatest risk they've taken in their careers...its scope has wider connotations but paradoxically, its subjects are narrower and less easy to identify...it's not a concept album...'Thick As Thieves' is possibly the best song Weller has *ever* written and the key to the album's theme...the song puts the others into perspective...the rest of the album Weller carries alone with his stunning vocals, chopping, abrupt and propulsive guitar and a batch of melodies and arrangements that put many of the songs on 'All Mod Cons' into the shade...more than ever, it's a one man band...'Setting Sons' is Weller's personal statement...the success of this album doesn't rely on familiarity and identification, but on his talent alone. It's Paul's best album yet; almost his first solo album too.'

Tony Stewart, NME.

'They've always settled for working within their own limits. There's no sense of ambition, no feeling that they've got to conquer the world by next Tuesday, Wednesday if they have a half day off on Saturday. So if The Clash are persistent under-achievers, The Jam are constant over-achievers...if you reach for the universe you'll almost certainly fall flat on your face now and again. If you set yourself modest targets you'll always get them but you won't get much further. Which is all by way of a perspective on this album. It's all good but none of it is great...as with all The Jam's best work, on first hearing it sounds perfect — it's only when you look close you see the holes...the real disappointment is that you feel that Weller doesn't quite understand that to perfect a song, you've got to take a lot more into consideration. And, of course, it doesn't help that he's as unwitty in his songs as he is in interviews...you pump them out with your usual panache and style — guitars ringing around a drum sound so hard you could cut diamonds with it and that whining Surrey accent — half guttersnipe, half confused adolescent...I found myself thinking of Ray Davies. There's the same wearing your suburban neuroses on your sleeve, the same lack of over-whelming confidence, the same disbelief that somebody is *paying* you to do this, and the same understanding that if you go so far, and no further, you'll never go wrong...long may Paul Weller have such modest aims.'

Pete Silverton, Sounds.

'Like Ray Davies of The Kinks, Paul Weller is obsessed with England...on 'Setting Sons' he takes a broader sweep all round...the result is a set of tunes of emotional depth and maturity...as on most of his compositions, here Weller is pointing his finger at the protagonist whilst accepting that he is merely a pawn in society's game...let's just say that 'Setting Sons' is a far more ambitious and adventurous project in every respect...the last great album of the Seventies.'

Record Mirror.

'Progression is the key word here, and this album is the evidence...the album reveals The Jam, and more pertinently Paul Weller, breaking away from the confinements of mod...he's coolly taking stock of all the evidence, and supplying us with his bleakest picture yet...by using a concept device, Weller is able to put forward two opposing points of view...outside of this concept, the picture is just as nasty...the band's ability to put together convincing sound-tracks for their scenarios...The Jam have never sounded better...Paul Weller is 21.'

Paolo Hewitt, Melody Maker.

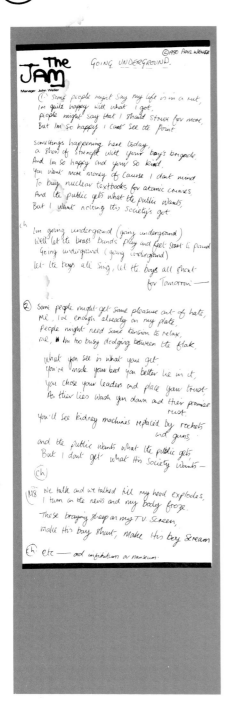

Throughout their career The Jam have always established something of a unique relationship with their audience. At first it was a cult affair, the likes of Shane and Adrian Thrills regularly turning up at their shows. As the band's popularity grew, they were forced into larger halls to accommodate their growing legion of admirers.

By doing this, The Jam strived harder to keep contact with their fans, played each show with as much conviction as possible, aware of their fan's expectations. With the success of 'Setting Sons', both artistically and commercially, those expectations grew to the point of fanaticism. After each show they would always drag themselves out of their dressing rooms to sign autographs.

'The guys have always done autographs,' says Kenny Wheeler, their tour manager since '78. 'They would like to do everybody, but then they don't get any time to themselves. I've seen them sign 300 to 400 autographs in a night. They're not robots and there are times when they're just not in the mood. I've seen them doing autographs two or three hours after a show.'

For Weller such contact was important for the group, not only to keep themselves accessible to their public, but also to ensure that The Jam never went the way of their predecessors. On that assumption, kids would be let into sound-checks, pushed through a back door if they were genuine fans unable to get tickets on the night.

It was on Weller's insistence that the people who came to see the group were treated as well as possible. 'We don't get a lot of trouble,' says Kenny, 'I used to say to the kids that nobody is here to hurt you. The worst place was the Rainbow, you'd get two kids jump on the stage but you'd never throw them out of the hall, they'd go straight back into the audience. When you do get them offstage they're like rabbits. You've got this big sod saying, don't hit me mister, and it's like the last thing you want to do. I think that if I ever hit a kid, I'd get the sack straight away; the band wouldn't stand for it.

'I've got to respect them for that. They realise that touring is about the kids, and they've always stuck to that. It even got to the point that when the band were onstage and there was a couple of kids by the stage door, you'd pull them in. The band put that sort of feeling into you. Whereas before, when working with a crew, you wouldn't really think of that. You realise after working with the band that that is what it's all about. I've told people to fuck off and had a right bollocking from Paul.'

After completing another major British tour — The Jam preferring to play two nights in a smaller place rather than a larger venue -climaxing with a three night stint at the Rainbow — the fanaticism they had engendered from their fans dramatically came to life with the release of their tenth single, 'Going Underground' c/w 'Dreams Of Children' on March 7th, 1981.

Intended as a double A-side, the group preferring the psychedelic overtones of 'Dreams' to the straight forward standard Jam sound of 'Underground', a pressing mix-up in France ensured that 'Underground' came out as the A-side. It didn't matter. 'Going Underground' entered the charts at number one, helped by some shrewd marketing by Polydor who released it on a Tuesday, thereby ensuring that it had a full week of sales as opposed to the three days a single is normally allowed.

In light of The Jam's success, such tactics seemed irrelevant; advance orders alone would have seen the single at number one.

'It's alright,' Weller says, 'if people want to drag that out, but the amount of people at our gigs, just the supporters, I think it would have happened anyway. It was the next logical step; everything was building and building and I knew that the actual support wasn't hyped. I certainly wouldn't care on a moral basis because as far as the music industry goes there ain't no morals.'

At the time of the success of 'Underground', phenomenal as it was, the group were in Los Angeles, staying at Hollywood's Sunset Marquee hotel. When the news came through, celebrations were the order of the night.

'The best party we had was when 'Going Underground' went to number one,' recalls Kenny Wheeler. 'I was sharing with John, and the party was in our room. So we stored all the gear away and ordered a lot of booze. During the party John was trying to phone home and someone cut the telephone wire. That was when I and various people got thrown in the pool. The next day we were actually barred from the Sunset Marquee.'

Out of the three Jam members, it was only Bruce who showed his feelings openly, although he wished — as did everyone else — that they were back in England. 'I mean,' says Bruce, 'obviously it was great with celebrations and everything, but it wasn't the same. I'd rather have been here and had the news, been home with people you knew and that sort of thing. You couldn't really believe it because you were so far away from it all.

'Probably, out of the three of us, I'm the only one who would like to get into celebratory drinks or something. I go out and I'm really over the moon about it and everybody can see it, but as for Paul I think he is, but he reacts in a different way. A few times I've thought to myself fuck, I'd have thought there'd be more of a reaction...'

Weller had, of course, been affected by the news, but as usual his feelings were mixed. 'I was a bit sort of shocked,' he says about his first number one. 'The other thing with me as well is that I try and keep calm about things like that because I get worried that I'm going to turn out like the rest of them. So I try to keep a little bit calm about it, look at it logically. At the same time, from my own point of view, my sort of ego, of course, I'm pleased.'

In fact, Paul Weller was close to tears the day he went to number one.

Now the obvious question was: how do you follow that? The adage that once you're at the top the only way to go is down never seemed more appropriate for The Jam.

'I don't know how much it affected Paul,' says Bruce Foxton. 'It probably did at the time and I know everybody was saying, what's going to happen now? Obviously we can't make number one every time. Oh dear, we're washed up and all that sort of business. But I think we knew that we could go on and still produce good records.

'After the initial feelings, we all reckoned we would not get a number one next time. I don't think we were too concerned about it after a while. It's nice to get your records in the charts, but we weren't primarily aiming at that all the time; we just wanted to release good songs. So we went back to that sort of attitude, just did the best we could every time.'

But the astonishing success of 'Underground' did cause Weller concern. 'I was really worried after that,' he admits. 'I see so many people who get number one records and then get fucked up. One hit wonders. I was scared we'd just slip up like that; which didn't happen because the band had such a tremendously strong feeling. But at the time I used to think to myself, what's going to happen if the next single doesn't go to number one? How am I going to feel? Which really, when it turned out, didn't matter. It was really okay.'

The band certainly had enough time to contemplate their next move. Always preferring the stage to either a studio or just sitting idly at home, their touring was extensive as they made progress in America and even added Japan to their growing list.

The constant waiting around in airports, hotels and dressing rooms gave Weller, as the songwriter, enough time to start sorting out new ideas. (A lot of Paul's early songs were written on tour.)

Nor did seeing so much of each other cause undue troubles. Although not as close as in the tempestuous early days of Michaels, there was still a discernible social chemistry between them, based mainly around Bruce and Paul.

'Rick in the last few years,' explains Paul, 'has become much more quieter. Basically you just live apart, different circle of friends and your own girlfriends, just doing different things. But we've always been pretty strong as a unit. If any of us needed support then I think we'd always be there, if it really came down to it. Particularly Bruce in that way. If there is any situation at all, he would never stop to think about it, he'd always help you. That's one of his best aspects.'

Their only problem, if it can be called that, was the amount of alcohol they were now consuming. Before each gig, Paul would regularly imbibe vodka or beer as a confidence booster, using it to calm his nerves.

'It wasn't alcoholic proportions, but I used to get regularly pissed,' Weller admits. 'On the early tours I would never drink before I went on stage, but I really started to enjoy things when 'All Mod Cons' was out, touring especially, so I started drinking again.

'I found out that when I used to drink I'd lose a bit of the nervousness and just generally enjoy things more. And I suppose the group started mixing together a little bit more; not so much Rick because he keeps himself to himself, but me and Bruce.'

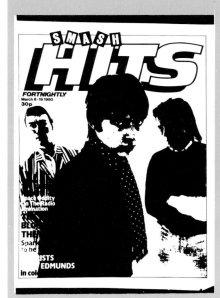

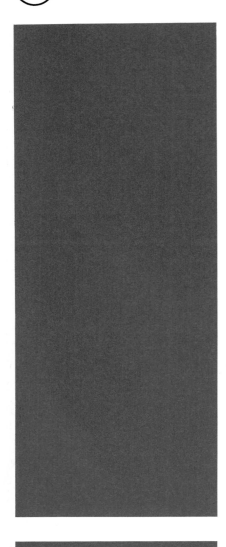

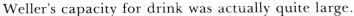

Weller's capacity for drink was actually quite large.

'I couldn't keep up with him,' says Kenny Wheeler. 'I don't know where he put it all. He used to drink coming back on a flight, say a 17 hour flight, and by the time you arrived he would have been drinking the whole flight. You've only got to walk through customs and if they know you're a band they'll turn you over for drugs. The good thing about this group is that nobody has ever been involved in that side. It's more booze.'

Hangovers amongst the group were commonplace, and on some occasions they even suffered further physical side effects. One time in France, for instance, Paul's stomach swelled up abnormally.

'My gut just came up like a hard boiled egg. You could actually ping it. So the doctor said to me no more beer for two weeks. Two weeks went by, stomach went down and I was back on the booze.'

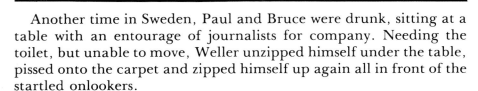

Another time in Sweden, Paul and Bruce were drunk, sitting at a table with an entourage of journalists for company. Needing the toilet, but unable to move, Weller unzipped himself under the table, pissed onto the carpet and zipped himself up again all in front of the startled onlookers.

Eventually something had to give.

One night after a show at London's Hammersmith Odeon, Rick Buckler and a tour manager called Dickie Bell sat down and consumed 34 bottles of wine between them. As Rick has a weak heart, most people with the group felt that he was actually close to death by the time the tour got to its next stop in Jersey. Pale and fragile, for a while it was touch and go. The experience hit home hard: Rick stopped drinking completely.

This dependence on alcohol in order to relax undoubtedly had its roots in the enormous pressure that now rested on the band's shoulders. The Jam (Weller especially) were pop stars to many, idols to thousands. Subsequently, the expectations of their audience would always be too high to be ever met satisfactorily.

All three of them stressed constantly that idolatry was not what they wanted. In interviews Weller would always disown any suggestion that he was a 'spokesman' or 'leader' for youth. To assume such a mantle would not only be pretentious but effectively categorise him neatly, thus denying him the freedom to do what he wanted to musically.

His motives for writing, however, still remained uncertain in his mind.

'I'm not sure what I try and do when I write a song,' he told *Melody Maker*. 'Mainly I write because I think a lot about things quite deeply, so therefore it's a means for me to express it and, without trying to sound too clichéd, that's what it is. But at the same time I try and write in a general sense so that other people . . . maybe it'll make them think as well.

'I think that we're successful and therefore we've got a certain responsibility, so if you're going to acknowledge that responsibility at all you might as well use it for the good. If you're influencing people, you might as well influence them for the better, because I've never asked for anyone to grab hold of my hair, scream and rip my buttons off. I'm not interested in any of that.'

Though Weller might not have been interested in fan hysteria, his audience certainly were. After a gig in Newcastle, a mob of kids, waiting outside the stage door, mobbed the group as they came out of the hall. In the ensuing confusion, two kids unwittingly pulled violently on Paul's scarf from either side and strangled him badly.

Another time, as the group got on their coach in Blackburn, the people watching broke into a song reminding Weller of films he'd seen of political rallies and of his own power as a pop musician.

'Some of it,' he states, 'gets to be a little like adulation, but at the same time a lot of them are such nice people as well. We always said we hate people idolising us and looking up to us, but even the people that come up and say things to you, you still respect them. On the one hand they can make you feel really uncomfortable and really crack you up, but at the same time I see the funny side of it.'

It wasn't unusual, in fact it became common practice, for groups of fans to follow The Jam all over the country or even in some cases to fly out to an American tour. In England, most fans would find the group's hotel and invade it, hoping for a chat, and then they'd come back after gigs to sleep in empty cleaning cupboards. The next day they would be making their way to the next gig, their devotion undiminished.

'If you want to keep as sane as possible you've got to try and remove yourself,' says Weller about fan worship. 'See how crazy it is and let it just wash over you a little bit. I also find it really funny because it's like living out a cliché or something.'

◆

What wasn't amusing was when over-zealous fans interfered in their personal lives.

'I used to live in this one flat in Pimlico,' Weller remembers, 'which was more or less opposite a school, which was a dopey move to make. Most of the kids round there knew where I lived and they really used to crack me up. I used to get people hanging about outside the windows at night and have to crawl around the room on all fours. It was horrible. And then people managed to get in the front door and knock on my flat door, all this sort of thing and it used to really freak me out.'

For Bruce and Rick the adulation was less intense, but still a tangible pressure. 'I don't think we've let it affect us as much as it could have done,' Bruce Foxton states. 'I don't think any of us have had big ideas that we wanted all the trimmings. We could have done, it's easy enough to get hold of, but we've all kept pretty level-headed about it.'

On a material level, all three members have never been ostentatious. Paul has always lived in tiny London flats, Bruce and Rick in houses that are small and comfortable. They seem to have been more bemused by their success than to have taken advantage of it, although they've obviously never resented it.

'I've never really taken the attitude that I was a famous person,' Rick says. 'I still get shocked when people come up and say, oh, you're so and so out of The Jam. At one particular point it did strike home as frightening, especially when you meet people after the shows and they won't come anywhere near you because they're scared of you.

'It's like the old thing that you always think Mick Jagger's seven foot tall but when you actually meet him he's five foot six or something. It's always other people's opinion of you that scares you more than being in the public eye, although it never really went to our heads. None of us started wearing glitter clothes and all that sort of caper.'

In fact, Weller had already taken advantage of the songwriting royalties that he was receiving and set up Riot Stories, his own publishing company. The first book to appear was *Notes From Hostile Street,* a collection of poems written by his old school friend and former member of the Jam, Dave Waller. Over the next few years it would be followed by a fanzine called *December Child,* which ran for two issues, a book on the Small Faces and another a collection of poems written by Aidan Cant.

Tragically, Dave Waller was never to write a second book. In 1982 he died from a drug overdose in Woking's Wheatsheaf Hotel, ironically one of the pubs he and Paul used to visit as teenagers.

'It didn't really shock me at all,' Paul says about Waller's death. 'It was bound to happen at some point anyway. We used to try and dissuade him from using drugs, but I think he had a bit of self-destruct in him. For some people, living is really painful, and I think Dave was a bit like that.'

This wasn't the first time that death had come close to Paul and the band. On a flight from Paris to Jersey the group narrowly escaped disaster.

'Not everybody likes flying,' explains Kenny Wheeler. 'Paul doesn't, Bruce doesn't and John's terrified. We were in a little twin-engined plane and it got to about 250 feet in the air when there was a 60 mile hour wind. This plane held about 40 people and it didn't only drop about 150 feet, it got blown sideways. Bruce doesn't smoke and he had a fag. John was downing large brandies and Paul and Gill were actually saying goodbye to each other. So much for jetting around the world.'

Another incident on a plane showed how tensions could run high. Flying into LA, Bruce and Rick fell out over a petty argument about a glass of vodka and went for each other's throats, throwing punches before they were pulled apart. After they'd landed and checked into the hotel, a record company representative approached Paul and Gill and passed the judgement that 'your bass player and drummer don't seem to like one another too much'.

Weller turned around to see Bruce and Rick fighting again in the hotel foyer...

These small outbursts on Bruce's behalf may have stemmed from his natural insecurity, a small part of his overall make up that Weller had already noticed.

'I think he's insecure,' says Paul. 'Like something would worry him and he'd just keep on and on about it. It would get everyone down a little bit, so arguments started that way. He'd panic about something and really go on about it.

Andy Hanson

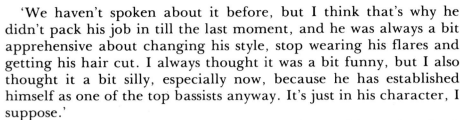

'We haven't spoken about it before, but I think that's why he didn't pack his job in till the last moment, and he was always a bit apprehensive about changing his style, stop wearing his flares and getting his hair cut. I always thought it was a bit funny, but I also thought it a bit silly, especially now, because he has established himself as one of the top bassists anyway. It's just in his character, I suppose.'

Where Rick or Paul managed to keep their emotions under check while touring, with Bruce his reactions would manifest themselves outwardly. After each show he would be ready for a drink or a club to help unwind, whilst Rick or Paul were just as content to enjoy a quiet night.

Sometimes there would be tantrums. 'There have been times when one or the other of them told me that they're going home,' says Ken Wheeler. 'Bruce said he wanted to go home in Canada. He scared the shit out of me because I went up to his room and his case and everything had gone. I really panicked and ran all over the hotel looking for him. He was calmly sitting downstairs eating breakfast, and there was me breaking into all kinds of sweat.'

By the time the group finally *did* arrive home, the ideas for their fifth LP were already forming in Weller's active mind. As a lot of his material is inspired by films, books and records, the influences he took into Virgin's Townhouse studio in Shepherd's Bush mirrored his then current interests.

For instance, in America he had been rediscovering The Beatles' 'Revolver' album and the debt can be clearly heard on 'Start!' which borrows the bass line from Lennon and McCartney's 'Taxman'.

Similarly, the ideas he wanted to explore lyrically sprang from the poems of Shelley and Blake he had been reading with growing interest, and indeed Shelley's *Mask Of Anarchy* is dutifully reprinted on the LP's back cover. Another book of major importance to Paul at this time was *Camelot And The Vision Of Albion* by Geoffrey Ash. This work in particular caught Weller's imagination.

'The ideas behind the 'Sound Affects' lyrics,' Weller admits, 'were influenced by Ash's book, which were that we had lost sight of our purpose and our goal as human beings, that material goals had hid the spiritual ones and clouded our perception. There were also religious overtones. I suppose, on reflection, the ideas and philosophies are quite 'heady' and 'hippyish', but it was just a phase I went through, basically because of the books I was reading — *Doors Of Perception* by Aldous Huxley was another — because they were concerned with mysticism and raising the spiritual and intellectual level of people.'

From this interest songs such as 'Set The House Ablaze' and 'Man In The Corner Shop' were written with the latter rating, in Weller's view, as one of the best pieces of music he's created.

'I love that song,' he says unashamedly. 'I think the melody is beautiful, and I wish it had been a single. I made it up on the spot at a rehearsal one day. I had some lyrics already, but I made the chords up out of thin air, and nearly all my best stuff is done like that.

'Once I get a feeling for the subject I'm writing about and a clear picture in my head of what I want to say, I find it quite easy. 'Man In The Corner Shop' is really English: the little corner shop owner struggling and hated by the struggling customers; and so it goes on. All one big unnecessary struggle and the factory nearby with its steam and go-home hooters, like the opening sequence of an early '60s black and white film.'

Again Weller, apart from his unabashed romanticism, was working best with his back against the wall, the pressure on him to deliver yet another batch of songs. Consequently he was writing in the studio or penning songs furiously at his London flat. 'That's Entertainment', for example, came about after a night on the booze.

Barry Plummer

'I wrote that,' Weller reveals, 'after coming back from the pub drunk with beery euphoria. I wrote seven verses, though I cut one of them the next day. The whole thing took about ten minutes because the words just rolled off my pen. I get moments like that when I just write reams and reams of stuff: songs, poems, thoughts in general. Most of it is crap, but I feel cleaned out after it and fresh. The tune to it I got later. It's a very simple tune that doesn't hide the lyrics and works well.'

Unlike the disjointed sessions for 'Setting Sons', Weller had adapted well to writing on the spot, enjoying the creative tension that it brought about in him. He was also writing differently, moving firmly away from his story type lyrics and setting down collages almost, utilising one line that would best evoke an image. 'Going Underground' was the first song he had written in this style, and on 'Sound Affects' he took the idiom a lot further.

But although the creative side was positive, the actual process of recording was worrying Weller. Producer Vic Coppersmith's slow laborious way of working was a complete anathema to Paul's instincts of immediacy and capturing the band as 'live' as possible.

'My constant thought,' Paul says, 'is always that it's us that's getting bland and smoothing out, and I've always been really worried about that. I didn't particularly like some of the things Vic was doing. Like his thing was always don't worry about the money, which I thought was easy for him to say, but that LP cost £120,000 to make which is a lot of fucking money: a ridiculous amount.

'Also, we weren't happy with the sound, and it was really slow working with Vic. He was good; some of the early things he arranged he did a really good job in shaping, but by that time I'd really learnt about arrangements and stuff. I think he was just a different sort of character, more laid back. Like he'd spend a whole day moving a drum kit into another studio just to find out it sounds the same, dopey things like that. People who listen at home to a record don't even think about it, they couldn't care less.

'That's the trouble with a lot of producers, big sort of bullshit about it. Stick a microphone on top of that, tie a kettle here, a sound that sounds amazing. . .it just comes out the fucking same anyway. As far as I can see, all that really matters is if the song is any good. If you've got a good song just play it straight and put the song first.'

After three trying months in the studio, 'Sound Affects' was finally completed. Once again The Jam, although pleased with the quality of the songs that they'd recorded, were disappointed with the LP's feel.

'In the end,' says Bruce Foxton, 'it lost it all on the overall sort of cut. We were well disappointed, and that's when we parted with Vic. I think he felt upset because it had gone on so long in the studio, and I think Vic felt he was rushed right at the end. It sounded flat. A lot of tracks were really quiet and we knew it was on the tape, it was all down. It just lost it from the multi-track to the actual vinyl. Also, we felt at that time we needed a change of producers. It was like five albums, and by that time we thought we could probably do a lot more ourselves.'

Three months before the release of the LP, The Jam's follow up single to 'Going Underground' was released.

One of only eight singles to have also appeared on an album, the critical reaction to 'Start!' — with that 'Taxman' bass line and harsh, clipped funk overtones, backed with the rough acoustic 'Liza Radley' featuring Foxton on accordion — was somewhat reserved with most writers dwelling on the overt Beatles influence. But Weller remained indifferent.

'I thought it was all a bit stupid,' he says. 'The riff thing doesn't bother me at all. I use anything and I don't really care whether people think it's credible or not, or if I'm credible to do it. If it suits me I do it, you know? People get a bit too precious about all that. They all come from somewhere. If you trace it, they all go back to those R&B records, so it doesn't really bother me.'

Entering the charts at number three, two weeks later 'Start!' was The Jam's second number one and confirmation of the dominant, unassailable position they now occupied.

Their worries about the success of 'Underground' and the affect it might have had on The Jam had proved unfounded. Up until their triumphant demise, there wouldn't be a pop group in Britain to touch them.

Returning to a simpler, less sophisticated sound, 'Sound Affects' remains The Jam's most durable LP, certainly one of their most cohesive statements. Although traces of Weller's influences occasionally flash through ('Start!' being the obvious example), the songwriting here borders on the great. The music, mainly melodic with frequent touches of inspiration, brilliantly captures Weller's fragmented words and thoughts, whether it be the gentleness of 'Monday' or the harsh brutal force of 'Set The House Ablaze'.

The first side in particular, despite the muted production, captures The Jam at their best. All the elements are there: Weller's voice alternating between desperation and anger, counterpointed beautifully by Foxton's cool harmonies. The urgent drama of the songs, be it a love song or a biting comment about people's loss of perception, crafted with an unerring intuition for pop's strengths.

It's only on the second side, following on from 'Dream Time' and the classic 'Man In The Corner Shop', that things pale. A filler instrumental and the superficial overtones of 'Boy About Town' (re-recorded to much greater effect for a *Flexipop* single) lower the standard before the bitter 'Scrapeaway' ends the LP on a jarring note.

But despite that, if sound does affect The Jam had easily made one of their best cases yet.

'Not another Jam album? Well, no actually. There's never been just another Jam album...this album takes the band forward...'Sound Affects' isn't a perfect Jam album, even if it is a great one...it's a brave departure and an earnest effort to break new ground...that dense heavy sound which found its climax in 'Going Underground' has been cut back, stripped down to only its most basic parts...instrumentation is stark, spare and hard...'Monday' is a beautiful love song that climbs up to classic status...these influences are only incorporated to enrich what's already there, and remain firmly subservient to Weller's own songwriting gifts...'That's Entertainment' must rate as one of Paul Weller's finest pieces to date...he's observing with more vivid descriptive ability than at any time previously...as always the view point is a humane, personalistic one...where 'Sound Affects' is good it's great, and where it's not so good it's still good...I've got 'Sound Affects' and I'm chuffed with it and all I want now is another Jam album.'

Paul Du Noyer, NME.

'The complexities start when I try to analyse just why I am not overwhelmed by this album...what I hear is a Jam album I respect, but don't necessarily like...I do not doubt Weller's sincerity — he has proved his ability at articulating the frustrations which form the sad foundation for this society...it is for them that Paul Weller speaks, it is why the song 'That's Entertainment' is one of Weller's finest ever efforts...Weller still has to prove that he has mastered those influences...Weller is still only 22 and this is the fifth album he has *created*...it's flawed but even in those flaws lie the seeds for the future, fascinating developments...Weller has set himself impressively high standards and 'Sound Affects' does not fully realise his capabilities...whilst I *admire* this album I do not like it. Not yet.'

Patrick Humphries, Melody Maker.

'They should have been shot down years ago! That they weren't is almost entirely due to the fact that Paul Weller talks to ordinary people in an extraordinary voice but minus the usual deceit or malice...Weller's humanism is as simple and direct as it is unaffected. He cares...in 'Sound Affects' they have made their best album yet...the barbs themselves aren't important, but what is, is the feel of challenge and commitment...as a result 'Sound Affects' is a truly stirring record...it brings the necessary orthodox of The Jam to a peak...the balance is magnificent, classical in design...a celebration of a liberating force in rock and roll (sound does affect!)...Side Two, for instance, opens viciously, polemically with typical English storyettes in taut fast music in the shape of 'Dream Time' and 'Man In The Corner Shop'...the second side is completed by the sheer classic 45 pop of 'Boy About Town' Dexys horns and all...it is heart music...from probably the last great English singles band, the most outspoken and rounded Jam LP yet.'

Dave McCullough, Sounds.

'It is hard not to feel the admiration, respect and, ultimately, the good-humoured jealousy intrinsic in any conversation regarding the ability, talent and maturity of Paul Weller...his acute ear for melody, his instinctive feel for the right emotional tinting, his powerful and relentless and mental and physical attack are the seeds that are brought to fruition by the drive of his rhythm section cohorts...'Sound Affects' finds Paul Weller's vision seeking retrenchment after the psychological full stop that was 'Setting Sons'...the sound still has the intrinsic Jam hallmarks...'That's Entertainment' is the set's high point, that angrily observes the mundane realities of eighties England...another fine Jam set that still eschews complacency but adds a new positive softness to the established abrasion, attack, rawness and life of previous outings.'

Mike Gardner, Record Mirror.

A month before the release of 'Sound Affects' Paul Weller finally met Pete Townshend at a specially arranged interview for *Melody Maker* at The Who's office in Wardour Street.

There had been previous attempts to meet. On Weller's 19th birthday two *NME* journalists, Tony Parsons and Julie Burchill, had driven him down to Townshend's Twickenham home only to find The Who guitarist out. They left him a copy of The Jam's debut LP and left.

Two weeks later, returning from a disastrous punk festival in France, a letter from Townshend was waiting for Paul at his family's house in Woking. Steve Carver was there at the time.

'Paul came in holding a whisky bottle,' Carver recalls, 'and he was pretty low. He opened this letter and it was from Townshend. It basically said: Dear Paul, sorry we didn't meet. Thanks for leaving the LP, I already had it. I think it's good, but then you know it's good.

'It actually drew comparisons with Townshend and Paul and it said that Paul was a big headed arrogant little bugger, and that's exactly how Townshend was at his age. It knocked Paul out.'

But when they eventually met, they discovered they had little in common. Townshend didn't like The Jam nor Paul The Who. They differed enormously over America, Paul stating that he didn't care if he ever went back, Townshend trying to stress the good parts of it and its people. They briefly touched on politics, Townshend's wider philosophies clashing pertinently with Weller's dogmatic approach, before Townshend finally concluded that Weller was 'a tougher nut than I ever was', and Paul advised him to drop old Who numbers from his set.

All in all it hadn't been a fruitful exchange of ideas, probably because Paul, now established as a major songwriter, no longer felt any empathy with The Who and couldn't relate in any way to the experiences Townshend had gone through in the '60s and '70s.

Not that Paul was particularly bothered by their lack of communication. With 'Sound Affects' rising rapidly to two in the charts, major tours of Britain, Europe, America and Japan now lay ahead of him as The Jam's popularity increased considerably.

A measure of the high esteem in which they were now held came with the sales of 'That's Entertainment'. Imported by their German label as a single, it reached 21 in the British charts, whilst in the prestigious *NME* Readers' Poll the group easily swept the board.

But despite all this, there was still discontent within the camp. Although their British tour had proved a personal success for the group, for Weller the deadening routine of constant writing and playing was beginning to plague him. This cycle, compounded by worries for Buckler's health, could only lead, in Weller's eyes, to staleness both in the studio and onstage.

Therefore, towards the end of the year, it was decided that the main part of 1981 was to be used for resting and that no LP would be recorded. The break had been on the cards for some time.

THE JAM
THAT'S ENTERTAINMENT

In a *Sounds* interview, John Weller had been quoted as saying, 'What I get frightened about sometimes is that maybe I've put a lot of pressure on three young guys. Then I feel a bit guilty about what we've created between us. But you get one magic night and that's all gone. Any dad has those feelings, if he's encouraged his son to be a solicitor and it doesn't work out. But The Jam have come to number one in the country and, better than that, they're still in the studio knocking out new numbers with the same zeal they always had.'

By the New Year, Weller had started involving himself in other projects, the first of these being television. Weller had written to BBC's *Something Else* programme suggesting a few ideas. They had responded by giving him a show to himself.

Enlisting the help of Steve Carver plus young writers he had come into contact with through Riot Stories, Weller made short films about class inequality and wrote the theme music.

In between the programme's creation, Weller also set up two record companies. One of them, Respond, first marketed through Polydor, would later make its own distinctive mark. The other, Jamming, was completely independent and handed over to a young Jam enthusiast called Tony Fletcher to run.

For Weller it was important that he used his money and power in such a manner, especially as he had always publicly claimed he would. Around the time of 'All Mod Cons' he had told *Zig Zag*, magazine in no uncertain terms that, 'I'm bursting with fucking ideas but it all takes money. It's a vicious circle. I can't do nothing until I've got the money. I'd love to have a publishing company so that I could publish young poets, people like Dave Waller.

'No one gives a crap about people like him. All they want to do is read Shelley and Keats, people like that. I'd love to have a record company to help young bands. But it all takes bread and right now I haven't got that sort of bread. But if I don't do that when I have got the bread then I'm the biggest cunt out.'

Ever conscious of hypocrisy (bordering on paranoia even) Weller had now achieved both aims. That the standard of the records and books he first published wasn't high didn't seem to bother him. The fact that he had kept his word was enough — for the time being anyway.

As for taking a rest, the compulsion to work had taken over again. Two major tours of Europe were completed before the group returned to record their twelfth single, 'Funeral Pyre' c/w 'Disguises'. The first single to bear The Jam's name on the songwriting credit, it was well below their usual high standard, any potential the song had buried by the welter of crushing bass, drums and feedback the band produced.

A disorderly single, the B side, an old Who song, compounded the problem further. Quite simply it was a mess.

'The reason behind it,' Weller explains of 'Pyre', 'was that at the time there were a lot of these really smooth records coming out, so we thought it would be good to do something rough. I don't know if it really came out that way. It was another period where I, as a songwriter, had exhausted all my supplies and ideas.'

Nevertheless, 'Funeral Pyre' reached four in the charts and The Jam, with the intention of playing venues they hadn't previously visited, undertook a mini British tour to support it. Oddly enough, they began their tour at the Rainbow in London, a venue they had headlined many times before. Weller acknowledged this onstage by cracking a joke about having a bed in the dressing room, but the set they delivered proved to be somewhat lacklustre, with 'Funeral Pyre' the only new song of the night.

Not a bad show by current standards, it was torn to pieces in the press next week, most pertinently by Adrian Thrills in the *NME*, who cited the show's orthodoxy — John Weller introducing them, the same old songs played — as cause for concern.

Although Weller privately agreed with him, he was furious that Thrills had rushed the piece into print before talking it over with him, a somewhat simplistic view considering the pressure of deadlines.

What Weller hadn't taken into account was the growing mood in London against conventional rock venues and bands. The emergence of a nightclub scene, best epitomised by clubs such as Le Beat Route and Club For Heroes, was quickly gaining popularity. Elitist and hedonistic, the frivolous attitudes of the people who ran and frequented these clubs was an insult to Weller, especially in the face of Britain's growing unemployment and declining economy. He quickly likened the scene to 'the last days of Rome', but couldn't help be attracted to the emphasis these clubs put on black music. Soon he began to check out these clubs, re-newing his acquaintance with Steve Strange, who he had first met in 1977.

Naturally, black music was hardly new to him. Back in '71 when he frequented the discos at Woking Football Club it was the only music played, although Paul completely ignored it at the time.

'At the time I detested it. I think a lot of people looked down on it. Not the kids who were actually involved in it, but a lot of people outside. Like black music itself was okay for 'kids' but it wasn't really serious music, and I must have had a bit of that in me. But I still used to buy all the latest releases because you had to. To keep up with everyone else.'

What most interested and intrigued Weller now, were the English groups who were beginning to incorporate these elements into their own music. He quickly grasped the fact that new possibilities were open, not only for The Jam, but for a fresh new scene.

The first signs of this interest came with the release of 'Absolute Beginners' c/w 'Tales From The Riverbank'. Weller had taken the A-side's title from a Colin MacInnes book which he hadn't then read, but was later to have a massive effect on him, and although 'Beginners' was not in the league of previous Jam singles, its prominent horn section and loose dance feel laid the seeds for a new direction.

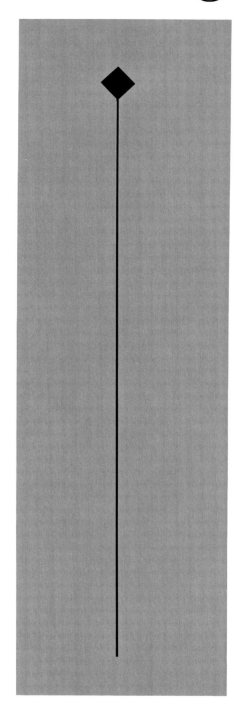

'Tales From The Riverbank' coincided with a slight psychedelic revival which had failed to take off. (Weller had tried to visit one of the clubs one night, but was turned away for not being dressed psychedelically enough.) Inspired by a piece of Woking woodland that Weller recalled from his childhood, 'Riverbank' was the best Jam song released that year and one which Paul, in retrospect, wished had been an A-side. He even held up the release of 'Beginners' to mix 'Riverbank' properly.

When the single entered the charts at its now customary high position, The Jam were preparing to enter Air Studios in Oxford Street to record their sixth LP. By now Weller had been completely taken by the revival of black music. He was buying loads of obscure Northern Soul records from specialist dealers, wishing he could have been part of the whole lifestyle as a youth and being fired by two records in particular: Pigbag's 'Papa's Got A Brand New Pigbag' and Spandau Ballet's 'Chant Number One'.

Janette Beckman.

Shooting the video for 'Funeral Pyre'

'I liked it. I thought it was really healthy,' he says of the fledgling funk movement. 'But I don't think anything came of it. It started to get less and less funky as far as I'm concerned. I thought 'Chant' was really good because it was a genuine English soul record; I thought it was a really important record. I was influenced by that.'

For Weller this emphasis on soul, coupled with the emergence of newer bands, was the push he needed to begin writing again. 'I like it when there's a lot of things going on, and a lot of *good* things going on, because that just inspires me; the fact that other people are doing it. It's like a real competition thing but in the nicest way possible, and I find that really healthy. It just gets boring when that's not happening, you get the whole area left open to you and I think it's important that everyone works together. I know I might seem the worst offender of slagging other groups off, but if it's something good I'll be the first to say so and encourage people.'

Sessions for 'The Gift' began in December with Pete Wilson producing. Weller had worked with Pete since 1980, but only on demos of his new songs. Wilson had impressed Weller with his quick methods of work and seemed more in tune with the sound Paul was after. Subsequently he was brought in as producer.

As usual Paul only had a few songs up his sleeve, but in the studio managed to conjure up one of his best ever, 'Ghosts'.

'Simplicity at its best,' he says of it. 'I made it up as I went along. Rick played a straight tapping beat and somehow I found that little riff and that was it.'

Recording schedules for the LP were split either side of Christmas '82, and as the days went by Weller became obsessed with the idea of making the best Jam LP ever. Convinced it was within their range, and determined to do it at all costs, Weller pushed himself and his companions as hard as he could during the day and, to relax, enjoyed a hectic social life by night. Eventually the lifestyle proved too much.

One morning at Air, after a heavy night out, Weller was playing pool. Suddenly he just started to fall to pieces. It was a mini-breakdown brought on him by a combination of work and drink.

'I just felt detached,' he says of the experience. 'I felt as if I was in a dream and that I would slip away and not be able to get back. It's a really horrible feeling and I think it was just stupid to go over the top. I've never been a real abuse person, and it wasn't only that but a combination of things. It was going out, pissing it up and the process of making 'The Gift' LP. I was really wound up, and I don't need that sort of pressure after a while. It's all right if it makes you a real 'artist' or something, but at the same time it does you in and I don't want to end up a basket case or something by the time I'm 25 or 26. I'd sooner do without that sort of pressure.'

Scared by the experience, which reminded Paul of the few times he'd taken acid, he immediately gave up drinking and cut down on his social life, preferring to concentrate solely on the work in hand, the sixth Jam LP.

With five songs now recorded, the group took a break to play four Christmas shows in London, two at the Michael Sobell Centre in Islington, and two at the Hammersmith Palais. It was important for Weller to present these shows along the lines of an old soul revue with different groups supporting each night and a Northern Soul DJ spinning discs. Unfortunately, the variety of the show bypassed a lot of the audience who greeted acts like Bananarama and The Questions with mindless chanting and abuse. This narrow-minded reaction to the group's attempts to offer something different obviously disappointed them, although there were some who appreciated it.

MCR PRESENTS

The JAM

Plus Special Guests
THE RUTS
Bananarama and Reaction
HAMMERSMITH PALAIS
Tuesday December 15th 7.00pm
Tickets £4.50 (Inc. VAT)
Admission will be refused to persons under 18

№ 274

Van Damme J.L.

Still, the sheep-like attitude of many of their fans caused concern within The Jam camp, especially with Paul, who had always stressed, ironically, the worth of the individual and who desperately needs an impetus to prove himself. If The Jam's audience, with their blind faith and adulation to everything he did, weren't providing that challenge, then it almost didn't seem worth carrying on.

Being teetotal also allowed Paul to see how absurd the drunken antics of his crowd were, especially when they spurned the attempts he had made to change the group's live act and their music. This desire to change was also causing friction within the studio. With most of their material, Paul has written it and then demo'd the song, playing all the parts himself, in order to give the group a clear idea of what he had in mind. Rick and Bruce would then take their parts and mould them to their own styles until eventually there are three distinct sounds.

On several of the songs for 'The Gift' — 'Just Who Is The Five O'Clock Hero' being the main example — Paul felt that his recorded demo version was better, with Rick's style of playing actually ruining the song.

Rick's version did appear on the album, but on that and a few other songs, Paul found himself disappointed with the overall feel.

'I think we could have done it,' says Weller, 'if we had dropped all the fucking ego thing and just concentrated on the songs, which to me is what counts. Because very few people say that's a really good guitar part or that was a good drum bit or bass bit; no-one cares and why should they? All I care about is the overall effect it has on people. That's what counts.'

Weller's fervent desire to make everything count also led to quarrels with Pete Wilson over the sound he was getting, although Paul does admit he may have let his determination go too far.

'I really wanted to put everything we had into the LP. I wanted it to be really, really important, and I think I drove it a little bit too hard. I think I made too much of it and blew it up in my own mind.'

Over Christmas, which Weller hates anyway, he had spent hours in his London flat working on the rest of the songs for the LP, and with the New Year a month old, The Jam's sixth LP was finally completed.

The recording didn't stop there. The group were soon back in the studio recording four cover versions of old soul records. Namely, Edwin Starr's 'War', Curtis Mayfield's 'Move On Up', James Brown's 'I Feel Good' and The Chi-lite's 'Stoned Out Of My Mind'. The Jam also recorded two Weller originals not on 'The Gift': 'The Great Depression' and the jazz influenced 'Shopping', both of which were to turn up later.

But although Weller had tried to push the music into a more soulful area, bringing in Keith Thomas and Steve Nichol on trumpet and saxophone respectively, after this bout of recording he was, unlike Bruce and Rick, mainly dissatisfied. To Bruce recording Paul's songs was a two-way thing, a give and take situation.

'There was a couple of songs,' he says, 'where we were saying, well, we think it's really good as it is, as it finished up on record, and Paul said he was disappointed cos he wanted it to feel more like the demo. But it was one of those things that you've got in your head, how you think it should sound and there was no way we could recreate exactly like it was on the demo. 'Transglobal Express' I thought was a really good song, and yet Paul didn't want to put it out at one point, didn't want it on the album and eventually I think it got harder and harder to interpret the feeling of how he wanted the stuff.'

As for Buckler, despite annoying Weller intensely when he remarked one day that the songs on the LP were 'not drummer's songs', he basically liked the work he'd done.

'I thoroughly enjoyed doing it,' he says. 'Believe it or not, it seemed harder for me to keep doing things simple and still try and make it sound interesting. I know on one or two of the tracks it never really worked . . . Or it did, but thinking back on it I suppose it's much the same with all the albums. You think you could have done this better or that better, but from that point of view I found it quite difficult. But it was a good challenge to try and keep everything back as far as possible without putting too much in. On one or two tracks there was a lot going on.'

'A Town Called Malice' was one of
The Jam's few international hits —
here they mime live! to it on Belgian
t.v.

Certainly there had been a distinct shift of style, with Paul exploring all forms of black music from funk, Northern Soul and even calypso where a steel band was brought in one day to play on a song called 'The Planner's Dream Goes Wrong'. Even so, it was slowly dawning on Weller that it might well be impossible to progress in the manner he had now set his heart on. Perhaps they had become so accustomed to each other, so rigid in their own particular style, that a loosening up and a complete change might well be impossible.

'We've never really sat down and talked about progression,' Weller admits. 'It's always happened. We've never really even sat and rehearsed or practised together. Every time we met up we just all of a sudden got a bit better. I think, inevitably, there has got to be a time when that stops happening.'

To wind down after 'The Gift', Paul took a week's holiday in the country with John and Kenny, driving around in a coach and visiting various Sussex beauty spots. Whilst there he learnt that The Jam's fourteenth single, 'Town Called Malice' c/w 'Precious' had entered the charts at number one, the second time they'd done that.

Obviously pleased by the news, he was also concerned by the increasingly frivolous nature of the newer groups emerging. Bands such as Haircut 100 and Duran Duran, with their pathetic pop tunes and nonsense lyrics, were an affront to his view of music, and he just hoped that the bitter words he spat out on 'Malice' over its obvious Motown beat and bass line would shake things up a little.

What he didn't know was that in 1982 he would cause the biggest shake up of them all.

Undoubtedly their most adventurous LP, it is paradoxically this very diversity with Weller juggling from English pop to soul music that gives 'The Gift' both its strength and weaknesses. At times — 'Ghosts', 'Precious', 'Trans-Global Express' and 'Town Called Malice' — the album works brilliantly within the parameters Weller set himself. But other songs veer from the mediocre 'Planner's Dream Goes Wrong', to the standard 'Happy Together' and the familiar 'Carnation'; which all unwittingly upset the balance, awkwardly placed within the overall direction.

Perhaps 'The Gift's' major revelation is Weller's voice which dominates as never before, a mark of the conviction he was attempting to give the album. Phrases such as 'soulful' and 'passionate' are used too frequently, but listen to him on 'Precious' (one of the few funk records sung as a soul classic) or 'Ghosts', and he's finally discovering the true range of his vocal power, able to reach a stirring emotional depth. The main influences are undoubtedly black (check the soul boy on the inner sleeve) but still containing Weller's ability to write unerringly about youth culture — 'Running On The Spot' — as well as tackle deeper subjects — 'Ghosts' — which previously he might have shied away from.

His political ideology also became clearer with the opinions expressed in 'Trans-Global Express' (the abdication of leaders in favour of workers' rule), but his writing still benefits the most from the poetic touches he adds to his reporting, even though it sometimes harks back to his old Sheerwater exercise book, as in the lines of 'Precious': *lonely as the moors on a winter's morning, quiet as the sea on a good calm night*.

Whatever, 'The Gift' contains a tangible presence that is both invigorating and mainly satisfactory. It reveals a push and energy that The Jam had never reached before and, despite its flaws, ranks with their very best work.

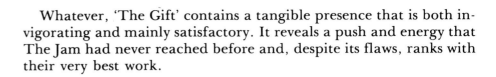

'Paul Weller writes and composes because he is a natural social commentator, a talented musician and emotionally articulate. . .this is a classic album opening slab of intense power and verve. . .real power pop. . .the only real disappointment is with 'Just Who Is The 5 O'Clock Hero'. . .a bit like a bottom heavy Stax-soul mix is 'Trans-Global Express', a swashbuckling rhythmic jamboree. . .at strategic points the whole thing melts into a rising tide of multiple repeat echo. . .'The Gift' is another brilliant Jam album. It will be proclaimed a masterpiece. It will be something for people in the Biz to clink cocktail glasses over. It will be bought in droves and treasured by fans. Thousands will hear it but how many will actually listen.'

Mick Sinclair, Sounds.

'After a year and a half in the desert, the three wise men return. . .fresh-faced 'innocents' may come and go but Paul Weller at 23 is the elder spokesman of British youth. . .the best Jam songs mix an angry kitchen-sink realism with a surging desire for a change. . .on 'The Gift' he finally steps off the fence and goes for *love* in the face of despair, and *intelligence* in the place of exhaustion. . .the musical range of 'The Gift' is wider than ever and The Jam's skills more developed. . .The Jam have retained their identity while enlarging it to include ringing brass work and best of all a bubbly happiness. . .Weller's understanding of dole-queue despair is equalled by his insistence on the value of the secret of the beat. . .Weller has no need to be intimidated by the triteness of recent fashions. Yet. . .I suspect he fears the problems raised by The Jam's superiority. . .the major dinosaur tendency on 'The Gift' is Weller's leanings to rather awkward and abstract lyrics. . .'Trans-Global Express' has Weller on the outside looking in, substituting sweeping statements for The Jam's usual faith. . .Weller and co keep their integrity by finding glamour no substitute for truth. . .Weller's earnest concern and occasional lyricism finds its perfect counterpart in the springing joy of sixties soul. . .thanks for 'The Gift'.'

Mark Cooper, Record Mirror.

''The Gift' is The Jam's ball of confusion. Though its purpose is laudable it's undermined by a failure to balance questions of style. . .what this record misses most is the cohesion and coherence of its predecessors. . .the tensions on which their records fed so brilliantly have, on 'The Gift', been pushed into irreconcilable extremes. It's an LP riven by frustration. . .the undercurrents that before were held together are now falling apart. Weller wants to be optimistic, but not escapist; he distrusts politics, but is drawn to political affairs (and can find little reason *there* to be optimistic); he seems tired of the old-style Jam music, rooted in '60s pop and soul, but knows of no better alternative, so ends up dabbling. . .stranger still comes on 'Trans-Global Express'. Lyrically this is the most radical statement The Jam have made, and its importance is emphasised on the inner sleeve. I suspect it's less a conversion to Marx than an update of the Shelley poem which appeared on the 'Sound Affects' sleeve, but it's all right-on stuff. How weird then that the lyrics are mixed so low they are practically inaudible, that what sounds like a potentially great Jam song is drowned in an excess of production tricks, electronic noises and jerky vocal bits. Coyness? Failure of nerve? I can't even guess...it's curious how Weller's political ideas, just like his music, can be traced back to the '60s...sadly the complexities and rich social detail that went into 'All Mod Cons' and 'Setting Sons' have largely been ditched in favour of such abstract simplifications...the one exception to this, and to all my criticisms...is 'Town Called Malice' a magnificent howl of outrage at Thatcherite Britain...I like 'Precious' for Weller's *great* singing, though it drags when it tries to become a funk workout. (Stay with *soul*, Paul)...the LP has a looser feel than previous Jam albums...The Jam have tried too hard to do too much without really having any stronger foundations than their own desperate desire to 'keep movin''. It's not enough, but I guess it shows they still care and for that, at least, I'm grateful.'

Graham Lock, NME.

'I'd guess that it's not much fun being Paul Weller, for all his success...Weller more than anyone is aware of the absurd tensions which his pop-star role automatically afflict him with...by a hideous irony, the supremely efficient Jam organisation would probably serve Thatcher as an excellent model for entrepreneurial organisation...Weller is virtually alone in this wonderful world of pop in conspicuously giving a damn. The effort nearly cripples him at times too, but when it works it's blinding. 'A Town Called Malice' for example...there's a strong streak of the romantic in Paul Weller. It inevitably tends to colour his perceptions and make his vision of class struggle and the indignity of labour seem oversimplified and at times almost Dickensian...despite the potency of some of the images it's only when Weller uses his imagination and not just his eyes that the song achieves anything more than impotent rage...musically The Jam are probably stronger than ever throughout 'The Gift'. There's more air and more room to breathe...and there has to be a special mention for 'Ghosts', probably the most haunting and haunted song Weller has ever written...in a couple of weeks I should know for sure whether 'The Gift' is a classic or merely a very good record. At the moment I can't get it off the turntable....*'thought that I was a devil?'* asks Weller in the opening track, a dogged statement of the will to win called 'Happy Together'. *'But I'm an angel waiting for my wings'.* Fine. Just stay away from those halos.'

Adam Sweeting, Melody Maker

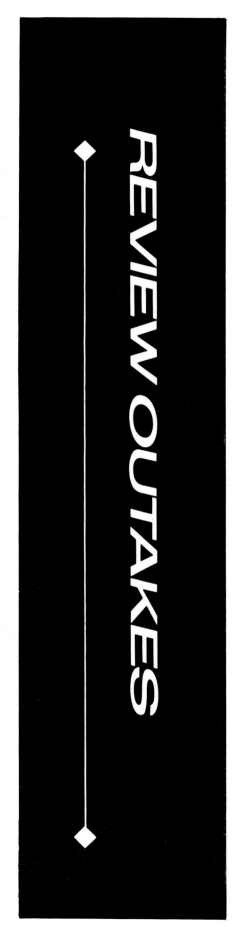

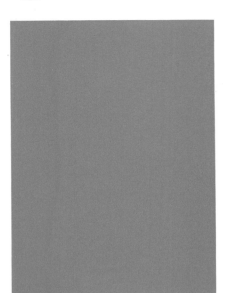

In October '82, prior to the troubled recordings of 'The Gift', The Jam publicly pledged their allegiance to a political movement, the Campaign For Nuclear Disarmament. At a CND rally near the Embankment in London, they organised a show featuring Jamming artists Zeitgeist and The Questions.

From the back of a lorry, The Jam also played two sets augmented by a horn section, bringing in Vaughn Toulouse, ex-Department S, to guest on vocals. The night before, the same line-up had made a guest appearance at the Gang Of Four's CND show at the Rainbow, running through cover versions of such tunes as Arthur Conley's 'Sweet Soul Music' and Sandie Shaw's 'Long Live Love'.

Weller's enthusiasm for CND was because it had one specific, vital aim to achieve, plus it had the potential to attract all ages and classes to its cause. Similarly, he had been impressed by the Animal Liberation Front (both Paul and Gill are strong vegetarians), and subsequently leaflets and the relevant literature were made available at every Jam gig.

Anton Corbijn

Compared to the night-clubbing character he'd been in the latter part of the previous year, the Paul Weller of 1982 was now undergoing a drastic change. He was slowly becoming disgusted with the stereotype behaviour he noted in a lot of young people. The boorish, macho mannerisms he'd chronicled in 'Saturday's Kids' held no charm for him and, after finally reading *Absolute Beginners* with its vivid descriptions of coffee bars, jazz clubs and emphasis on youth, he began to immerse himself in a cleaner lifestyle.

Contemporary pop music was also annoying him, the childish nature perpetuated by the likes of Altered Images or the over-blown pomposity of ABC filling him with a determination to become even more outspoken in his views and music. Slowly but surely, the whole rock culture he had become a small part of, was becoming an enemy to fight and consequently he was portrayed in the medium as a humourless pop figure, unable to grin a little, let alone crack a smile.

In the programme for the Trans-Global Express Tour, Weller wrote with biting anger, 'I want this tour to be the shake-up music needs, I want it to cut through the increasing fucking apathy...' But it never could be. The Jam were simply too huge to make the kind of impact Weller dreamed of.

'That's because I think things had become too big,' remarks Paul 'Although I've always said that the majority of people really understand it, but sometimes it gets a bit like blind faith, you know. Also I didn't think the playing on that tour had any kind of real finesse or any kind of grace either. The songs didn't really acquire that. They should have been a bit more subtle. It was our inability to modify our songs or start again, break up everything we've established and start again, which I think we could have done, but it's hard to say. Maybe you just get to a peak and that's it.

'It could have been a lot looser, especially with the brass section, we could have made it really loose and made it more enjoyable for all of us.'

For Bruce Foxton matters were now a little disconcerting as he was the only member of the group who drank or wanted a good night out after a show.

'Well, if you don't drink, it doesn't help,' he explains. 'If you're going to go out socialising you're on different levels. I mean, one of you is getting well-lubricated and the others are pretty serious about everything. I'd like to see them relax. They both seem, particularly Paul, tense — more so since they've given up drink.'

The Trans-Global Tour took four months to complete, taking in Britain, Europe, Canada, America and Japan. Everywhere the band played, the signs were encouraging. In Canada they headlined a major outdoor festival. In Los Angeles and New York shows had to be added, and 'The Gift' stayed in the American charts for an impressive number of weeks, testimony to the popularity the band were now enjoying in the States.

Previous tours there had been a disappointment and sometimes not even worth the cost of the airfare. Since 'Setting Sons', with its rich, thick sound, however, the States had started to take note of the Woking Wonders.

Steve Rapport

With the arrival of 'The Gift', things finally seemed to be moving their way. Despite the elements of their music which Americans in particular had found hard to take (Weller's typically English vocal, his infatuation with class struggle and the brutal feel to a lot of the songs), there now seemed to be an audience ready to accept them on their own terms. Indeed, when The Jam made an appearance at Tower Records in Los Angeles there were near riots outside as they spent four hours signing autographs.

Even so, touring was killing them.

'The tours just became more and more boring,' Weller admits, 'mainly due to our jaded attitude. If it wasn't Bruce moaning it was me or Rick or, on that tour, one of the brass players. It was terrible and in the end I just thought what a boring bunch of ungrateful gits! We stopped enjoying it and I couldn't stand the tantrums anymore. There were so many childish arguments that I think we all had enough, but no one would admit it. Bruce's attitude in particular would piss everyone off because he would always be griping about something or the other. Which was a shame because really he is a good bloke.'

Incidents such as Joe Awome, one of the Jam's security men, being mistakenly arrested in Sweden hadn't helped either, and with Weller frustrated by the music they were playing each night it wasn't a happy group that finally arrived home. Bruce Foxton had also compounded the problem by innocently remarking in a *Melody Maker* interview, conducted in Japan, that he was amazed by Paul's work rate. Talking about 'The Gift', he expressed astonishment at Paul's prolific ability. Whilst he had been at home partying, Paul had produced enough songs to fill an LP.

When the story ran, Weller instantly became annoyed at the implication that he knocked off songs a dozen to the minute 'like some factory line', and that Bruce didn't take into account the enormous effort he expends on one song alone.

Further on in the interview, Foxton also remarked on the band's disappointment with their English fans, 'it makes you wonder how many of them are actually listening', and the need for the group to have a good think about their future. 'We're going to have to sit down and work it all out,' said Foxton.

The meeting Foxton hoped for took place. But the subject discussed was entirely different to the one he had in mind.

In the summer of 1982, Paul and Gill took a two-week holiday in Italy, staying in Naples and Rome before catching the Orient Express home. When they got back to their London flat, Paul Weller had finally made his mind up. After eight years together as a group, he was going to leave The Jam, walk out on Britain's most successful group in which he had played the main part.

The first to know was his father. John Weller's immediate reaction was to talk Paul out of it. But he knew deep down that once his son had made a decision there would be no turning back.

'There have been times,' says John, 'when we've had ups and downs, but because you're the older person I think you've got to swallow your pride. I try and look at it from his point of view and I've never really been what they call an old fart. I'm like one of the youngsters. Let's face it, today's youth is tomorrow's world and what the fucking hell am I going to do about it?

'But I did feel sad about it because I started it. It's no good saying Paul hasn't got the talent because he has, and without it the ongoing situation wouldn't have been maintained. But I did start it off and it's like the end of something that wasn't really finished. My dream was to get them really fucking massive. I would have loved to see them playing Madison Square Garden and all that. I still would. But it never came about because Paul didn't want to play venues that big. That's really what it was.

'It was no good me putting it together because I knew that he didn't really want to do it, so in a sense I was a little bit constricted. Another manager who wasn't involved personally would have said that's what we're doing and it probably would have worked. Maybe, because I was his father, that was one of the holdbacks. But with regard to them playing prestigious venues, they never really achieved quite what I wanted to see. In the UK they did, but not really abroad. Filling Madison Square Garden, I would have loved that. They couldn't have got any higher and that would have done me.'

After informing John of his decision, Paul was now faced with the unpleasant task of letting Bruce and Rick know. At first he was hesitant about doing so. A secret farewell tour had to be arranged and, knowing Bruce's volatile temper, his reaction could easily upset any future plans.

Eventually, after about a month of brooding, The Jam began recording their fifteenth single, a ballad Paul had written on his return from touring. (In the same amount of time he'd penned three other new songs. 'Solid Bond In Your Heart', 'Beat Surrender' and 'Dr Love' a song he gave to Bananarama for their debut LP.) Entitled, ironically enough, 'The Bitterest Pill' they were at Marcus Studios recording when a meeting was called.

Immediately Bruce Foxton suspected something was up. 'We were just mucking around with some demos,' he remembers. 'John was there, Paul hadn't arrived, and John was saying I know Paul wants a meeting with us all. We very rarely had meetings. I mean, obviously we had meetings when we were going on tour to see where we wanted to play, and we'd go through it as we always have done, so I knew something was happening.

'But I thought it was just going to be a break or more recording and leaving the touring out for a while because we had spoken briefly about it in Japan.'

Instead, Paul told Bruce and Rick he was leaving the band. For a moment they were utterly shattered by the news, unable to comprehend the implications of it all.

'There wasn't a lot to say,' remarks Bruce. 'Everyone was really stunned. I think all I managed to say was like a bit drastic, why don't you leave it for six months? If you want to unwind or you want to do other projects. . . I mean, you could see that he was getting involved with his own label and publishing and other bands, so I expected he might be doing other things with them. So I thought he might have gone off on that for a while and give The Jam a break.'

For Rick the impact was just as great. 'It was something we'd all been involved in most of our adult lives,' he reflects, 'and it was almost like losing a limb at first. You think, oh God, and start throwing fits of depression, but after a couple of days of just thinking about the situation it seemed to come clear that it was probably the right thing to do.

'My own personal opinion is that it was a little premature, but if Paul was unhappy then there was no point in keeping it going just for the sake of me or Bruce. It just wouldn't have worked, so you resign yourself to the fact and think a bit more positively about it.'

If anyone, it was Bruce Foxton who was hit hardest by the news. After completing 'The Bitterest Pill' which took two recorded attempts to get right, The Jam, under the direction of young artisan Pete Barrett, filmed a video for the single in and around London one weekend. After waiting around for what seemed like ages, Bruce finally lost his temper and stormed off the set on Sunday night and a Polydor employee was quickly drafted in to take his place. The next day Bruce rang up and informed the group that he wasn't doing the British tour that had been set up. Then he slammed the phone down.

Faced with the prospect of losing thousands of pounds by having to break contracts with promoters all over the country, the idea of getting ex-Sex Pistol Glen Matlock in to replace him was mooted. Matlock and Weller go back a long way. After Glen had left the Pistols and formed The Rich Kids, he'd asked Paul to leave The Jam and go with him. Paul declined the offer. Jimmy Pursey also approached Paul once with the idea of forming a 'punk supergroup', somehow Weller had managed to turn that one down too...

Two days later Foxton finally relented. 'It's going to sound childish,' the bassist admits, 'but I didn't want to tour or anything. I just thought, fuck it I can't go through with it. All the enthusiasm had gone and I couldn't get to grips with the fact that we were splitting up. Obviously I was wondering what the feelings would be like onstage. I had two or three days to cool down and come to grips with it, chatting with Pat my girlfriend and eventually thought, well, the fans would like to see us once more and that kind of business.'

Foxton wasn't the only one feeling the strain. Another blazing row with Gill had resulted in Paul moving out of his flat and taking refuge in a hotel for a couple of days to let matters simmer down. The feelings within The Jam weren't exactly positive and Weller, typically, just wanted to move on to his projects and lay The Jam to rest.

On September 3rd 'The Bitterest Pill' was released and the critical reaction underlined to Weller that the group were in a cul-de-sac because of their 'serious' image. To him 'Pill' was an obviously funny song. Unfortunately no one got the joke.

'People say we haven't got a sense of humour in our songs,' Weller complains, 'but even if we do it people wouldn't get it anyway because they're not looking for it. And that pisses me off. People take so many things literally. I just don't think they look far enough into the songs, but I suppose it does boil down to your sense of humour. I mean, some of the lines in 'Bitterest Pill' were just obviously over the top and overly dramatic. To me they were obviously funny. Like the last verse in it: *'Autumn's breeze blows down summer's leaves'*, and no one has really picked up on it. Some of them wankers wrote, well it's Weller's sojourn into introspection, all this crap, and it means nothing. Maybe in some ways we might even have put ourselves into that position, I'm not really sure.'

'The Bitterest Pill' c/w 'Alfie' and 'The Fever' was certainly an ambitious song from the start. Their first single as a ballad with strings, it featured a duet between Paul and Jenny from The Belle Stars. (He'd originally wanted to use the girl who sang on Defunkt's 'The Razor's Edge' but she wasn't available.) The humour in it, although not overt, is further disguised by Weller's impassioned vocal which blinds the listener to the words and forces you to concentrate more on the song's *feel*.

Reaching two in the charts, the band's impending split was still being kept secret. To avoid hysteria, it was decided that they should play their Farewell Tour to unsuspecting audiences and as it turned out, the tour proved to be one of the most enjoyable they'd undertaken. With Bruce and Rick having partly come to terms with the split, any bad feelings were quickly shelved for the tour's duration.

'Probably one of the best tours we'd done for ages,' recalls Foxton, 'because there was no animosity between us, and maybe it was just a big weight off Paul's shoulders. He'd obviously thought about it for a long while and looking at him onstage I felt that he was back into it 100 per cent. He was really giving his all, whereas before you could see that he was getting more and more pissed off with every gig he was doing and I actually expected some sort of break because of that.

'I thought to myself, what was the fucking point in touring every night if it makes you miserable? I mean, he obviously didn't want to be there. Things were getting him down more and more and it does rub off, it rubs off on all of us. It's got to and you do think lets chuck it in, this is ridiculous.

'So that was really creeping in, but then this last tour, once he'd told us he wanted to leave, the pressure was gone and by going out and playing the old numbers again it was real fun.'

Ditching the horn section for this tour, the band were augmented onstage by a keyboard player, Jimmy Telford, and two back-up vocalists, Afrodiziac. Mainly they played as a three-piece delivering two-hour long sets to enthusiastic crowds everywhere.

But if the tour was a refreshing success psychologically, Weller certainly didn't enjoy it physically. He had struggled through most of the dates with a painful rash of shingles on his stomach, and it was his painful condition which caused them to cancel their European tour.

Back home they already had two recorded songs, 'Beat Surrender' and 'Solid Bond In Your Heart' as choices for their final single. After much deliberation 'Surrender' was picked. It was an ironic choice of title but hadn't been written with the split in mind, which was still very much a secret to the public. Only a few close friends knew of it with Weller intending to announce it officially on *The Tube,* a new Channel 4 pop programme that had specifically invited the group onto their debut show.

But a month before the show, the news leaked out. The first rumour appeared in *Sounds* one week as a gossip piece. The next week both London's *Evening Standard* and *Record Mirror* were running the story as 'official'. How they got hold of it no one is too sure, although one theory is that one of the road crew leaked it to a journalist friend.

Rob Hall

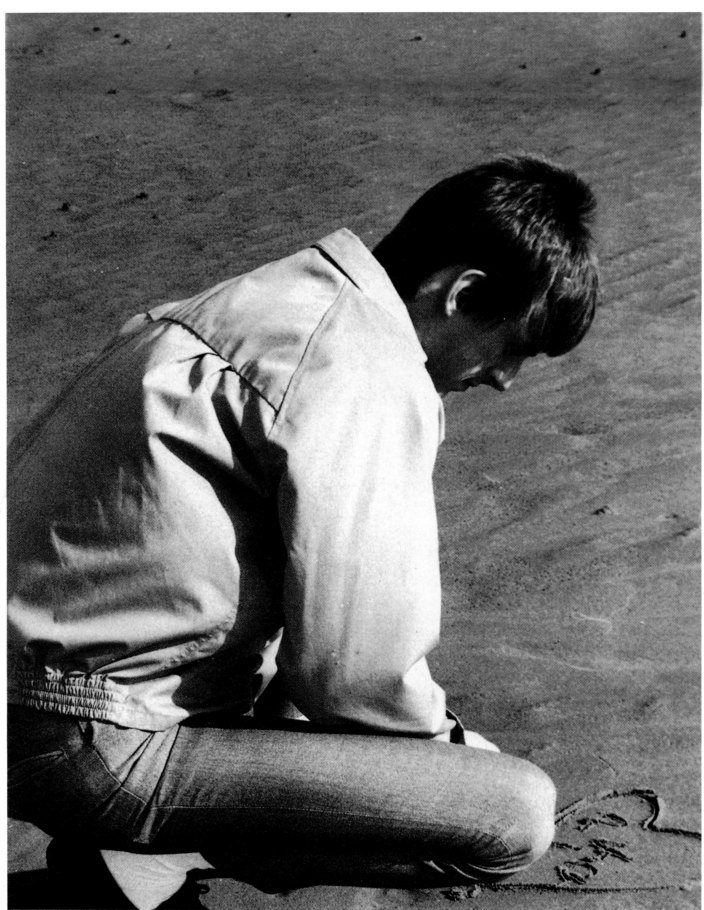

Love letters in the sand

In the light of so much speculation, the group decided to come clean and a press handout was issued to all the papers. Bruce Foxton, however, was still clinging to the notion that it still might not happen.

'I didn't even tell my mum about the split until after we had done the tour,' he says. 'In the back of my mind I was just hoping that Paul would have a change of heart, although I didn't think he would. Paul is pretty set in his ways and once he makes his mind up he's very strong-minded.

'Anyway, just as it started to leak out I thought I'd better go round and tell my parents because they'd be well chuffed if they had read about it or heard about it from someone else. I didn't want to tell anybody about it. Just lived with it for a month or so, just me and Pat, every minute of the day thinking about it.'

For Rick Buckler, the split now meant he had to look long and hard at his future. 'One thing that was scarey,' Rick reveals, 'was that it hardened my attitude towards money. I've never really given a fuck about it, but only because I knew it was there. Obviously, now I've got to start thinking about earning for myself, so, in that respect, it's hardened my attitude. None of us are left with financial problems, we don't owe anybody anything which is good. John made sure that we were alright. I think that would have made the situation worse if we'd had nothing, if we had gone willy-nilly with our money in the past then it would have been a real culture shock for us to suddenly realise that there wasn't anything else. But none of us live extravagant lifestyles.

'We've all got a house and a car and furniture and carpets and all the bills are paid. We never used to take three months holiday in Hawaii. There's a little man inside me which said I wish you fucking had, but on the other hand what you've never seen you never miss do you?'

While Rick and Bruce were contemplating their futures, Paul was busily making plans of his own. With the weight of The Jam removed, he was now given a new lease of life, presented with a new important challenge to face up to.

'It really dawned on me,' he told *Melody Maker,* 'how secure the situation was, the fact that we could go on for the next ten years making records, getting hits, getting bigger and bigger. That frightened me because I realised we were going to end up like all the rest of those groups. If we carried on for the sake of it, it would just bring our name down. I don't like the thought of The Jam when we're around 30 and old and embarrassing because I think we've always stood for youth.'

Weller's natural love for music, his awesome desire to make it meaningful and relevant, his admitted chauvinism about youth, the belief he has in keeping things as pure and as powerful as they can be — all these elements had led to his decision to break with The Jam.

Proud of what he had achieved with the group, aware of the impact they had made upon thousands of teenagers, in a positive *and* negative sense, he wanted The Jam to stand as an example of how a group could be dignified and strong and not be tainted by old age or music business excesses.

He'd also decided to become something of a soul musician and realised that such an ambition could not be realised with The Jam. Tied down by the serious image he had acquired over the years, the massive expectations of his audience and the heavy responsibility that went with it, also meant that he had never been able to relax and enjoy the fruits of his labour. Constant pressures on him, either to write songs or tour, had finally taken its toll over the six years. Rock music held no charm for him now and he was quickly seeing through its transparency.

'It's totally redundant,' he told *MM*. 'It's just a big empty fucking vehicle for nothing. It's like the emperor's new clothes. It's got nothing at all.'

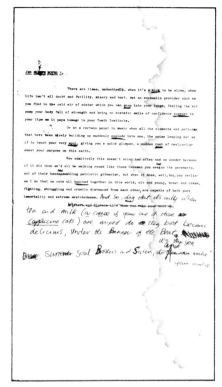

The potency inherent in soul music was far more appealing to him. 'I still believe in music,' he added. 'I think you have to hit people with feelings. It's like when I think of all the greatest songs, my favourite songs, they're always these melancholy ballads, a Smokey Robinson song or The Four Tops, and you realise it's because they hadn't got any politics at all. You don't even *think* about the lyrics, it's just the feeling that gets you. I think it's better if you try and appeal to people's emotions.'

To avoid the problems he had encountered before, Weller decided that his future career would now be with a loose nucleus of musicians. Simultaneously he would involve himself far more with the running of Respond and Riot Stories. As a result, he withdrew his support from Jamming, partly because it was running at a loss and partly because he wanted to concentrate solely on Respond. Before any of these ideas could reach fruition, however, there was still the final part of The Jam's career to put to rest.

On November 26th, 1982, 'Beat Surrender' c/w 'Shopping' and the three soul covers the band had recorded earlier that year, was released. One of their most powerful singles, 'Surrender' is undoubtedly a classic Jam 45, thriving on an intoxicating energy and excitement.

Backed up by Afrodiziac and Tracie (who would later go on to reach success herself on Paul's Respond label), Weller's vocal is one of the finest he's ever recorded and it was fitting that for the third time in their career, the single should enter the charts at number one. In keeping with Weller's new train of thought musically, the lyrics were once again a mixture of views.

'The ideas always get mixed up,' says Weller of his writing. 'Nothing is really direct or as set as some of the early ones. Like, I can get four or five different themes in the song. I think that 'Surrender' is about a lot of things. It's about sex, well more of an asexual thing. Mainly seeing young boys and girls in and around the West End, the way they look and the energy there. So it's partly about that, and also about music. Some of the lines in it are about what music can do for you, get you off your arse and make you feel really powerful.'

The flip side 'Shopping', a slow jazzy tune, indicated Weller's new direction for the future, but before he could truly branch out it was decided to issue the final Jam LP, a live one chronicling their chequered career. Out of the 21 tapes Polydor presented Paul with, he settled on 14 songs from different stages of the group's life, stole a line from a James Brown song for the album's title and on December 3rd, 'Dig The New Breed' was released.

Ironically, the person who stopped it from entering the charts at number one was John Lennon, one of Paul's few heroes. That week he sold 50 more copies than The Jam.

'If I'd known that', remarked Weller, 'I'd have gone out and bought the other 51 myself.'

As far as live albums go, 'Dig The New Breed' is a fair enough representation of how The Jam were onstage, a ragged, intense sound of frustration and fury which reaches a peak on 'Set The House Ablaze' and 'Private Hell', and is smoothed out by including such a song as the Beatley 'It's Too Bad'. In between these two stools there's touching versions of 'Ghosts', a bludgeoning treatment of Eddie Floyd's 'Big Bird', the raw intensity of 'That's Entertainment' and 'Dreams of Children', the excitement of 'All Mod Cons' seguing into 'To Be Someone', the mediocre 'Standards' and powerful renditions of 'Going Underground', 'In The Crowd', 'In The City' and 'Start!'.

The choice of songs seems to represent more Weller's own personal memories of The Jam rather than conventional ideas of representing a group. But with the material available, any number of permutations would probably have sufficed.

The title is positive, but the album throws no clear light on the group's work, no one direction or statement emerges from it. Perhaps that's where its charm lays.

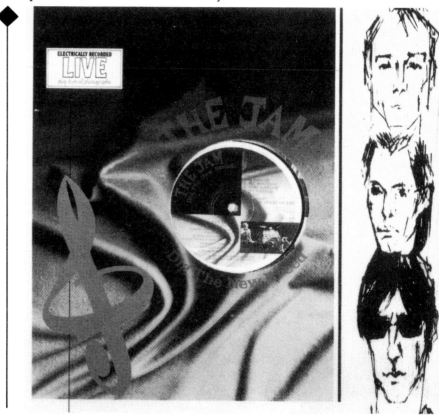

'Inevitably this record is more of a souvenir than an art statement. . .the last Jam album is a gift for the fans, a spur for the memory more than a necessary record. . .the 14 songs remind you that The Jam live were always a punk band. . .this record captures much of the abrupt fervour of those early Jam gigs. . .some of your favourites will be here, some won't. . .few of the songs improve with live performance, they merely gain in attack what they lose in subtlety. . .the laying to rest of The Jam is the first exciting demise of a band since that of The Sex Pistols. . .this record is not as exciting as Weller's decision but it's a nice reminder. Thanks for the memories.'

Mark Cooper, Record Mirror.

REVIEW OUTAKES

'TAKE NO HEROES! Some moments are to be treasured forever...looking back it is the rise and rise of The Jam that is, more than anything else, a towering beacon of hope against the present gloomy musical backdrop...what is INSPIRING is that The Jam have progressed so much and changed attitudes so visibly...Weller has shifted massively, away from the early casual youth anthems that pinpointed the division as young v. old, t'wards songs that deal with far greater ogres, far greater issues — an issue as great as 'class'...the point is this — a change in attitudes is HOPE. And if you sneer at hope, you sneer at progress...meantimes The Jam have split and left us with the hippest of anthems...an album that frames all those nights of fire and accelerated passions, 14 tracks that chart The Jam's heady progress...the difference between The Jam and all the hopeless pop ephemeralities is the difference between a (red) harrington and an anorak...The Jam have STYLE and SIGNIFICANCE...'Dig The New Breed' is a sharp package...mebbe the last *authentic* mod record...there will be greater moments, sure, but for the while this one is great enough. Sublime sound, sublime vision — The Jam were the best. TAKE INSPIRATION!'

X. Moore, NME.

'How much can you say anymore about a live album?...Very obviously 'Dig The New Breed' is a straight, no surprises 'Live Album'...this is an affair between The Jam and their fans...within their own circle The Jam were too straight...'Dig' is, if anything, a dead end of a record justly placed at the end of a career...perhaps the sole blemish of The Jam's career (horrible word!) was that the conservative streak of the Wellerian politik came too much to the fore...it is, in truth, thrash and no tension...celebratory anger does not get captured well...we await a weirder re-emergent Weller, breeding the new dig.'

Dave McCullough, Sounds.

'Faced with this, the final Jam LP, the temptation to wax lyrical (not to mention boringly), about the group, their music and What It All Meant to thousands of people is obvious...they may have been 'about' a lot of things — some great music, youth excitement and trust — but as I remember it, The Jam always tried to look forward rather than backward...words like honesty and integrity are words that have no real significance to the music business, but The Jam always tried to breathe life into them...The Jam always made more sense live simply because their belief and passion could be given proper breathing space...it is fitting that The Jam should bow out with a live LP, and one that takes a few chances, refuses to fit into the established mould of greatest hits regurgitated ad infinitum...quite simply we shan't see their like again for a long time.'

Paolo Hewitt, Melody Maker.

Anton Corbijn

Finally, the last concerts. A standing, moving ovation at Glasgow *before* the group play a note. A brilliant set at Guildford, preceded by five nights at the massive Wembley Stadium. But with the end in sight no one is callous enough to argue the merits of playing there.

The Jam, boosted by horns, keyboard players and singers, cope magnificently in the cavernous hall, their committed playing translating powerfully to the crowds, the reception they receive a touching vindication of their achievements.

They play the last show on a dreary day in Brighton. Weller aloof from the emotions that are running high ('Why should I be cut up? I'm proud of what I've achieved'.) and more concerned with the future — thinking about The Questions and Tracie, two acts he's already signed to his Respond label, and what his next move will be.

His two companions are still slightly confused; more so Bruce Foxton. 'All these dates have been brilliant,' he remarks. 'They really have, and the feeling from everyone is so electric. One minute you're on cloud nine and the next you're right down. It really is weird and it's a strange thing to handle. I still haven't got to grips with it yet.'

Indeed, it will take Foxton the longest to realise The Jam are no longer a part of his future. As for the last show, it's a ragged set that could never live up to its status, although fittingly their last song together is 'The Gift', a celebration of hope and optimism.

The Jam legacy, however, still remains. In the next year all 16 Jam singles would be re-released and all 16 would enter the charts together. In fact, since the split, it would seem that Weller has never been more popular, although in hindsight it's not hard to understand why.

His songs aroused, through their direct, straightforward comments, a massive response from mainly young people who recognised in his work familiar thoughts and feelings. Weller wrote mainly about youth, British working class youth. It was these topics that absorbed him, although The Jam were never a 'political' band in the full sense of the word. Weller's dabblings in politics didn't really come to fruition until 'Setting Sons' where he began to make more sense of the complexities of the system he despised.

His songs are mainly about himself. Either they're personal reflections or else private fantasies channelled through characters like 'Billy Hunt'. Certainly there are political overtones to his work. Songs such as 'Trans-Global Express' and 'Little Boy Soldiers' are prime examples. But where he hit home hardest was when he focused solely on his and other people's lives, forever questioning the conditioning, ideals and ambitions that society foists upon us.

This ability to pinpoint weaknesses came from Weller's natural frustration at the scheme of things. He views the world in black and white, which is why he never fully played out a clichéd rock star's lifestyle. He knew to do so would be to commit one of the worst sins in his book, hypocrisy, and thus The Jam, publicly at least, did their best to remain unaffected by their powerful position.

To the cynics, it all sounds a bit too good to be true. No one is perfect, and undoubtedly The Jam made a few mistakes in their time. 'The Modern World' LP: compromising by having swear words cut out of singles; playing cavernous arenas like Bingley Hall; and, with hindsight, making dreadful statements upon their earlier records.

WEMBLEY ARENA

HARVEY GOLDSMITH ENTERTAINMENTS &
MCP PRESENT

THE JAM

**plus Special Guests
in Concert**

Saturday, 4th December, '82
at 7.15 p.m. (Doors open 6.30 p.m.)

**GRAND TIER SOUTH
£6.00**

TO BE RETAINED   See conditions on back

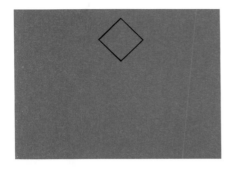

Weller admits to these faults: 'I don't think The Jam, as such, could be taken seriously or intelligently until 'All Mod Cons'. And at least it displays a human frailty that is encouraging in the light of so many 'perfect' stars.

Similarly they could be picked on for their very orthodox methods: their choice of venues, the presentation of the shows, their unadventurous image all lacked imagination in many cases, although paradoxically it was this straightahead approach that appealed to so many people.

Andy Rosen

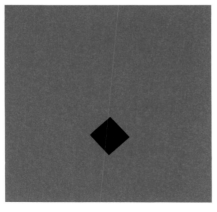

It's fair to say that Weller also felt stifled by these confines. Indeed, his decision to leave the group partly stemmed from this frustration and the knowledge that he was growing away from his audience. As one who recognises the value of change, Weller had increasingly divorced himself from the working class stereotype. He doesn't drink, patronise pubs or make much of a noise these days.

Instead, he now looks to the European lifestyle for direction, hangs out a lot in cafés and lives a much quieter, cleaner lifestyle. Thus to his contemporaries he's either a shining light of example — 'Cool clean and hard *Record Mirror* called me. I like that' — or to his detractors a dour puritan, cynically exploiting the masses. Neither assessment is true, although his ability as a songwriter is beyond question. The majority of his work still stands today as memorable and, at times, classic examples of pop's possibilities.

Jam records always possessed an urgent need to infiltrate people's lives, be noticed above the others —'Wake up a sleeping nation,' as Peter Townshend wrote in London's *Time Out* magazine — and challenge in every way possible. Weller never dictated, rather he charged in asking all kinds of questions, determined to get a response.

Thus The Jam served as a welcome antidote to pop's usual superficiality, and Weller constantly remained armed against criticism on an ideological level. All the ideals he stated in public were fulfilled and he has, on the quiet, helped out all kinds of bands or political causes.

Ultimately, though, it was the response he received from his audience, the realisation that The Jam actually meant more than a scrawled autograph or a bedroom poster, that gave him his proudest moments.

Unequivocally, he states: 'I'm proud of what we've done and when I read letters from all sorts of different people, even more so. It's not them stroking your ego, it's good to know that you can mean that much to so many people and not just be another group in a great big line of them. I mean, I thought the best letter was that one in *NME* that said The Jam were our Elvis or our Beatles for our generation and thankfully they're not going to be our Rolling Stones. I thought that was really great and I've had loads of letters like that. Not just recently, but over the last six years.

'Just to be able to communicate with people, I'm really proud of that. It's probably my proudest achievement, that the songs have been really respected and actually mean something to people. There's a lot of things which are good for your ego, but the things that stay with you and have really lasted are those things, where you know you've really got through and really made contact with people.

'I think for any sort of writer it's got to be the thing you aim for. Sometimes I wonder how many letters groups like ABC get about their songs. It just wouldn't mean anything to me. What's the point in having number one records if that's all it is? Anyone can fucking do that. It's when you really break all that down, when it becomes more than music or another group or another record, when you become something bigger and stronger than that.

'That's what I think is different, that's why The Jam have always been different. I can't really think of many groups that have done that, not in the same way, not in the same uncompromising manner. I mean, The Beatles did it in some ways, but they really had to compromise. We never did that; The Jam *never* did that.'

One night, a silver haired man, an ex-boxer and builder by trade with a family to support, sat down and made a list of everything he wanted his 14-year-old son to achieve. As the years passed and his son's group began to take off he began to tick off each achievement until one day there was only one ambition left on John Weller's piece of paper: to become bigger than The Beatles.

The Jam never achieved that. But in the end they became something far more vital, far more pure and far more worthwhile.

Discography

Singles

Singles	Date	HCP
In The City/Takin' My Love	May '77	#40
All Around The World/Carnaby Street	Jul '77	#13
The Modern World/Sweet Soul Music (Live)/		
Back In My Arms Again (Live)/Bricks and Mortar (Live)	Nov '77	#36
News Of The World/Aunties and Uncles (Impulsive Youths)/Innocent Man	Mar '78	#27
David Watts/'A' Bomb In Wardour Street	Aug '78	#25
Down In The Tube Station At Midnight/So Sad About Us/The Night	Oct '78	#15
Strange Town/The Butterfly Collector	Mar '79	#15
When You're Young/Smithers-Jones	Aug '79	#17
Eton Rifles/See Saw	Nov '79	#3
Going Underground/The Dreams Of Children		
Going Underground/The Dreams Of Children/		
Away From The Numbers (Live)/The Modern World (Live)/		
Down In The Tube Station At Midnight (Live) [7" Double pack]	Mar '80	#1
Start/Liza Radley	Aug '80	#1
That's Entertainment/		
Down In The Tube Station At Midnight (live) [German Import]	Feb '81	#21
Funeral Pyre/Disguises	Jun '81	#4
Absolute Beginners/Tales From The River Bank	Oct '81	#4
Town Called Malice/Precious		
Town Called Malice (Live)/Precious(Extended Version) [12"]	Feb '82	#1
Just Who Is The Five O'Clock Hero/		
War/The Great Depression [Dutch Import 7"&12"]	Jul '82	#8
The Bitterest Pill (I Ever Had To Swallow)/Pity Poor Alfie/Fever	Sep '82	#2
Beat Surrender/Shopping		
Beat Surrender/Shopping/Move On Up/		
Stoned Out Of My Mind/War [7" Double Pack &12"]	Dec '82	#1

Albums

Albums	Date	HCP
In The City	May '77	#20
This Is The Modern World	Nov '77	#22
All Mod Cons	Nov '78	#6
Setting Sons	Nov '79	#4
Sound Affects	Dec '80	#2
The Gift	Mar '82	#1
Dig The New Breed	Dec '82	#2
Snap	Oct '83	#2
Greatest Hits	Jul '91	#2
Extras	Apr '92	#15
Live Jam	Oct '93	#28
The Jam Collection	Jul '96	

NB: HCP = Highest Chart Position

April 1980
Strange Town, All Around The World, The Modern World, News of the World and **David Watts** all re-entered the Top 75 following the release of **Going Underground**.

Jan/Feb 1983
Following the band's split, all of the singles were re-issued and all entered the Top 75, with the exception of **Funeral Pyre** and **Absolute Beginners**.

June 1991
That's Entertainment was re-released with its original B-side, **Down In The Tube Station At Midnight(Live)**. The 12" and CD formats also included the live version of **Town Called Malice**.

June 1992
Dreams of Children was re-released as a single in its own right minus the original double A-side, **Going Underground**. Instead it was coupled with **Away From The Numbers** (Live) and on the 12" and CD, **The Modern World**.

With thanks to John Devlin